RESCUING AFGHANISTAN

William Maley is professor and director of the Asia-Pacific College of Diplomacy at the Australian National University. He has served as a visiting professor at the Russian Diplomatic Academy, a visiting fellow at the Centre for the Study of Public Policy at the University of Strathclyde, and a visiting research fellow in the Refugee Studies Programme at Oxford University.

A regular visitor to Afghanistan, he is author of *The Afghanistan Wars* (2002); edited *Fundamentalism Reborn? Afghanistan and the Taliban* (1998, 2001); co-authored *Regime Change in Afghanistan: Foreign Intervention and the Politics of Legitimacy* (1991) and *Political Order in Post-Communist Afghanistan* (1992); and co-edited *The Soviet Withdrawal from Afghanistan* (1989) and *From Civil Strife to Civil Society: Civil and Military Responsibilities in Disrupted States* (2003).

Crises in World Politics

TARAK BARKAWI
JAMES MAYALL
BRENDAN SIMMS
editors

GÉRARD PRUNIER
Darfur—the Ambiguous Genocide

MARK ETHERINGTON
Revolt on the Tigris

FAISAL DEVJI
Landscapes of the Jihad

AHMED HASHIM
Insurgency and Counter-Insurgency in Iraq

ERIC HERRING & GLEN RANGWALA
Iraq in Fragments—the Occupation and its Legacy

STEVE TATHAM
Losing Arab Hearts and Minds

IAIN KING & WHIT MASON
Peace at any Price—How the World Failed Kosovo

Rescuing Afghanistan

WILLIAM MALEY

HURST & COMPANY, LONDON

Published in the United Kingdom by
C. Hurst & Co. (Publishers) Ltd
41 Great Russell Street, London WC1B 3PL
© William Maley, 2006
All rights reserved.
Printed in India

A catalogue record for this volume is available at
the British Library.

ISBN 1-85065-846-3

Contents

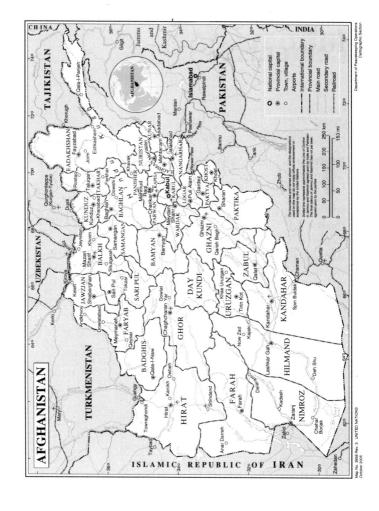

Introduction

This is largely a tale of two Septembers, and of the years between them. In September 2001, the charismatic leader of Afghanistan's anti-Taliban forces, Ahmad Shah Massoud, was murdered by Arab assassins, and terrorists killed thousands of people, of many nationalities, in the World Trade Center and the Pentagon. Four years later, in September 2005, Afghanistan witnessed elections for a new parliament, amid hopes that the country would finally recover from decades of misery and suffering. Over intervening period a remarkable endeavour had taken place, commencing with the onset of "Operation Enduring Freedom" on 7 October 2001, in which the international community, Afghan leaders, and millions of ordinary Afghans worked to pull their country from the abyss into which it had been thrust. How successful this rescue mission will prove to have been only time will tell, but already important lessons can be learned from examining its course.

Afghanistan is a landlocked Central Asian state, the population of which is overwhelmingly Muslim but segmented in complex ways on ethnic, sectarian, and regional grounds. Its emergence is typically dated from the commencement of the rule of Ahmad Shah Durrani in 1747; it began to assume more of the trappings of a modern state during the rule of Abdul Rahman Khan from 1880 to 1901; and it became fully independent in 1919.[1] It has a reputation for turbulence, partly because of the vivid writings of British poets and storytellers who depicted unhappy encounters with

7

Afghan rulers and tribesmen in the days of the British Raj. This reputation is not altogether deserved. For nearly 50 years before a communist coup in April 1978 fatally disrupted the rhythm of social and political life, Afghanistan was one of the most peaceful countries in Asia. Its equilibrium, however, was fragile: the over-throw of the King of Afghanistan, Muhammad Zahir Shah, by his cousin Muhammad Daoud in July 1973 not only displaced the monarch from the throne he had occupied for nearly 40 years, but highlighted fissures that were developing in the political elite, divi-sions that culminated in a bloody Marxist takeover less than five years later.[2] The tragedy of the 1978 coup was then greatly com-pounded by the effects over the following years of various self-interested interventions by Afghanistan's neighbours. In December 1979, the Soviet Union invaded Afghanistan to replace the brutal dictator Hafizullah Amin with a Marxist more to its liking, the pliable puppet Babrak Karmal, inaugurating nearly a decade of sorrow for both sides, which came to an end only with the withdrawal of Soviet troops in February 1989.[3] In its own inter-est, Pakistan channelled western support to radical elements of the resistance (Mujahideen) movement, and finally, following the dis-integration of the communist regime in April 1992, intervened more directly from 1994, using as its tool first the Hezb-e Islami (Party of Islam) headed by the ruthless Gulbuddin Hekmatyar, and then the Taliban movement.

As a result of these external influences, ordinary Afghans fell victim to extreme and even obscurantist ideological forces whose orientations were sharply at odds with the dominant strands of thought within Afghanistan's kaleidoscope of micro-societies. Marxism-Leninism held no appeal for most Afghans, who saw it as a threat to their faith and way of life. Yet while Islam became the foundational element of resistance to the Soviet presence,[4] radical Islamism also surfaced, with Pakistani backing, as a threat to the pragmatic, society-based Islam of the bulk of the population.[5] The collapse of the Soviet Union at the end of 1991 eliminated Marx-ism as a factor in Afghan political life, although one of the four key figures in the 1978 coup, Sayid Muhammad Gulabzoi, survived to be elected to the parliament in 2005. But radical Islamism, as represented principally by Hekmatyar's Hezb-e Islami and ultimately Osama Bin Laden's terrorist al-Qaeda organisation, proved a noxious weed, as did the neofundamentalist Taliban with whom Bin Laden so comfortably aligned himself. Hekmatyar's rocketing of Kabul, designed to ensure that no one else could rule if he did not, destroyed much of the southern part of the city between 1992 and 1995, while the Taliban supplied a totalitarian mindset, albeit without the bureaucratic agencies to give it full effect. Dealing with the accumulated legacy of this extremism is part of the challenge of drawing Afghanistan back into the community of nations.

Afghanistan's need for assistance can hardly be overstated. Following the 1978 coup, Afghans suffered a series of hammer blows from which any people would find it difficult to recover. Many hundreds of thousands were killed during the period of communist rule, and by early 1990, some 6.2 million Afghans were refugees in Pakistan and Iran, out of a pre-invasion population estimated at only 13.05 million.[6] The state largely collapsed, and a range of new forces emerged, some of them profoundly unappetising. Agriculture, from which the bulk of the population had derived its livelihood, suffered severe damage in many parts of the country, and any semblance of a "national" market was lost in favour of substantial regional autarky. With the destruction of educational institutions and the flight of teachers and other educated professionals from the country, a generation of students was lost. And as if this were not bad enough, the scattering of antipersonnel mines in many parts of the country made roads impassable, fields unusable, and dwellings uninhabitable. As the writer Gavin Bell put it, it was as if someone had dropped a bomb in the Garden of Eden.[7]

On top of all these hardships was the misery brought by the Taliban. A motley, pathogenic, anti-modernist force, drawn overwhelmingly from the Pushtun ethnic group and instrumentalised by irresponsible components of the Pakistani state, the Taliban offered repression without hope of recovery from Afghanistan's travails, and weirdly painted the desert over which they presided as a model of Islamic rectitude.[8] They managed to prevail not because they enjoyed substantial popular support throughout Afghanistan, but on account of their trusty lifeline from Pakistan and the sheer exhaustion of the war-weary Afghans whom they were seeking to dominate. Comprehensively ignorant of the wider world, the Taliban increasingly took their lead from al-Qaeda, and then were sucked into a crisis they could not control. Yet if the 11 September 2001 attacks put the Taliban in an impossible position, for other Afghans they offered an unexpected opportunity to reconnect with the wider world. This came when the overthrow of the Taliban regime in November 2001 left the international community with the task of helping to put something workable in its place. Whether consciously planned or not, a rescue mission was under way.

The meaning of "rescue"

When it occurred, Operation Enduring Freedom was not especially controversial, certainly far less so than the March 2003 invasion of Iraq. As the political scientist Barnett R. Rubin has put it, "The military intervention to defeat the Taliban and al-Qaeda enjoyed broad legitimacy both internationally and domestically in Afghanistan."[9] Operation Enduring Freedom, and the events that followed it, nonetheless can be interpreted in a number of ways. One view of these events sees them as a form of "humanitarian intervention,"[10] where military power is forcibly deployed on the territory of a state without the consent of its government, with the dominant purpose of realising some humanitarian objective. Operation Enduring Freedom did not fit this model, for two reasons. First, the objective of helping the Afghan people was secondary to the objective of obliterating a concrete terrorist threat.[11] The suffering of the Afghans was apparent long before the United States chose to do anything about it. Second, the Taliban had failed spectacularly in their efforts to secure recognition as a "government": only Pakistan, Saudi Arabia and the United Arab Emirates had ever granted them recognition, and Afghanistan's United Nations seat remained in the hands of the anti-Taliban "Rabbani government,"[12] which was happy to see international assistance finally materialise.

Another approach might see Enduring Freedom and its after-math as manifestations of the international "responsibility to protect" endorsed by the International Commission on Interven-tion and State Sovereignty in an influential report finalised just one week before the operation commenced. The commission's disag-gregation of a responsibility to protect into specific responsibilities to prevent, react, and rebuild certainly pointed to significant over-lap between its concerns and the objectives of the US-led Coalition forces.[13] Again, however, the practical reality is that protection of the Afghans was not the principal objective of the operation, as their need for protection from predatory forces had been apparent for years before the United States chose to react; and the US and its allies did not seek to depict what they were doing as a discharge of moral responsibility, but as an exercise of self-defence.

This brings us to the idea of rescue. To rescue is to "set free or deliver… from attack, harm or custody,"[14] and it has a direct Per-sian equivalent, *nejat dadan*, which literally means "to give deliverance." Applied to world affairs, this term usually refers to missions to extract the nationals of a state from a threatening situ-ation in which they have become entangled in some other country. But the term does not presuppose the motivations that must underpin a party's actions. It is understandable – indeed, desirable – that for an intervention to be dubbed "humanitarian" it must be driven primarily by humanitarian motives. Yet it is useful also to have a terminology to label actions and processes that may be ini-tiated in self-defence and pursued primarily out of self-interest while at the same time bringing humanitarian benefits. The notion of a rescue mission captures this complex mixture of underlying motives.

Furthermore, those who mount a rescue are typically and rightly seen as having ongoing responsibilities towards those whom they have aided. These need not be open-ended, but little credit goes to those who toss aside people whom they have only recent pulled to safety. Such responsibilities apply to states as much as they do to people. And a rescue mission need not simply involve two parties, an active rescuer and a passive "rescuee." When the

Titanic struck an iceberg on the night of 15 April 1912 it was not just the crew of the *Carpathia* who contributed to the survival of 705 of the *Titanic*'s passengers and crew; many survivors owed their lives to fellow crew and passengers of the vessel on which they had been travelling. Similarly, the attempt to rescue Afghanistan has involved not just the wider world, but the people of Afghanistan itself. For all these reasons, mounting a rescue mission can be an admirable step to take.

That said, the term can also have an additional element: some forms of rescue are distinctly patronising.[15] Those who see themselves as rescuers may view those whom they aid as passive recipients of their goodwill – and in doing so, deny the beneficiaries their capacity to be active agents. This can lead down a road to ruin, where "textbook" models of political transition are applied without much sensitivity to local conditions, questions of the long-term sustainability of change are substantially neglected, and local actors are accorded marginal political roles and minimal control of resources. Rescue missions thus can have both positive and negative dimensions, and in discussing efforts to rescue Afghanistan it is important that both be weighed in the balance. At the end of the day, there may be more than a tinge of irony in the idea of a "rescue mission," especially if significant pathologies can be linked to the way in which it was carried out.

In the following six chapters I look in detail at how events have unfolded since late 2001. Chapter one outlines the problems that those engaged in "rescuing" Afghanistan have had to confront. Chapter two addresses the problem of reconstituting the political system, and creating a legitimate state. Chapter three is concerned with the fundamental issue of security. Chapter four turns to the means by which human development can be promoted, examining options for improving education and health, the threat posed by illicit activities, various visions of Afghanistan's economic future, and the place of international assistance. Chapter five looks to Afghanistan's relationships with the wider world and the importance of reintegrating Afghanistan as a "normal" state. As well as identifying both positive and negative factors shaping Afghanistan's social and political trajectories, the final chapter takes up some difficult issues by which Afghanistan continues to be affected: the dilemmas of protecting human rights and delivering transitional justice; the importance of ongoing international attention; and, above all, the need for vigilance.

In an earlier book, I recorded an old Kabul proverb that there is a path to the top of even the highest mountain.[16] Since the overthrow of the Taliban, the people of Afghanistan have been treading that path. There have been many obstacles along the way, the pathway is steep, and the summit has not yet been reached. Indeed, disaster could still strike the procession. Yet in spite of all these difficulties, and with the support of much of the wider world, the people of Afghanistan have forged ahead with enthusiasm and great courage. I hope that this small book will serve in part as a tribute to their efforts.

CHAPTER 1

The nature of Afghanistan's problems

Afghanistan's problems are enormous, and any attempt to sum them up will necessarily be fragmentary and superficial. The full tale of the decades of disruption will never be told, but each family has its own story of deprivation, of displacement, of despair. Nonetheless, to understand what rescuing Afghanistan entails, it is necessary to begin by identifying some key challenges, and that is the focus of this chapter.

Transition plans do not appear on a blank page. One of the most frustrating difficulties in addressing the problems of severely disrupted states is that conditions at the outset are often so unpromising. Afghanistan faces this problem to a particularly acute degree. It is a desperately poor country, although strong norms of social solidarity have sometimes disguised the scale of its development problems to casual outside observers. It has also been ravaged by decades of conflict. As a result of these years of armed struggle, the tasks involved in rescuing the country are daunting, and there is no easy point of departure for addressing them.[1] Talk of "post-conflict transition" has a hollow ring when conflict continues to blight the lives of Afghans in some parts of the country. The notion of "transition" evokes images of smooth, unidirectional change when the ground reality is more one of progress (either smooth or sporadic) in some geographical regions and spheres of activity, and regress in others.[2] Responding to Afghanistan's problems is further complicated by the need to rebuild basic institutions through which they can be addressed, and by the difficulty of working out which problems to address first when all of them are serious and seem to cry out for immediate attention.

State disruption

The starting point for virtually all discussion of Afghanistan's problems is the disruption of the Afghan state. The term "state" here refers not to a territorial unit, but to a particular configuration of instrumentalities: Afghanistan might well be seen as an example of what the international relations scholar Robert H. Jackson has called a "quasi-state," enjoying a high level of "juridical sovereignty" (indicated by the broad international acceptance of its existence within its present boundaries) but a low level of "empirical sovereignty" (as measured by the capacities of government instrumentalities).[3] In practice. a state consists of ministries, departments, agencies, and a range of related bodies, reflecting a degree of institutional development in a polity. As one writer has put it, "for there to be a state, political power must be vested in and exercised through a set of purposefully contrived arrangements – a body of rules, a series of roles, a body of resources – seen as concerned with and committed to a distinctive, unified and unifying set of interests and purposes."[4] More abstractly, the political scientist Joel S. Migdal has defined the state as "a field of power marked by the use and threat of violence and shaped by (1) *the image of a coherent, controlling organization in a territory, which is a representation of the people bounded by that territory*, and (2) *the actual practices of its multiple parts*."[5] When the image or reality of a "coherent, controlling organization" is undermined, the state is at risk; when both are significantly eroded, then the state can properly be described as disrupted.

Such erosion can occur for either of two reasons, and frequently from a combination of both.[6] The first is a breakdown of state *capacity*. This can flow from a number of causes, including a fall in the volume of resources available to fund state activities, and severe divisions among those in charge of different components of the state. The second is a decline in the *legitimacy* of the state. The logic of legitimacy was expressed with notable clarity by Edmund Burke in his 1775 *Speech on Moving Resolutions for Conciliation with the Colonies*: "the use of force alone is but *temporary*. It may subdue for a moment; but it does not remove the necessity of subduing again: and a nation is not governed, which is perpetually to be conquered."[7] States rarely rule purely by force: for a state to function effectively, at the very least it must be able to secure the active support of people to play key roles in its administration.[8] An unexpected decline in state capacity has the potential to undermine legitimacy, with the likely result of accentuated popular discontent and elite fragmentation. The strength of states can be measured in terms of their possession of various capacities. Migdal has identified these as including "the capacities to *penetrate* society, *regulate* social relationships, *extract* resources, and *appropriate* or use resources in determined ways."[9]

In a number of these spheres, the Afghan state before 1978 was relatively weak, and survived because its leaders prudently avoided initiatives likely to provoke strong opposition. Outside the cities, the agencies of the state were ubiquitous but somewhat ramshackle – "weak links on a rusty chain," as one observer put it.[10] The bureaucracy was riddled with nepotism,[11] and this was particularly a problem in the armed forces where young non-elite members of the Pushtun ethnic group in the officer corps "found their road to promotion and choice assignments blocked by the old inner circle of Pushtuns with close connections to the royal family."[12] The inauguration of a new and notably democratic constitution in 1964 promoted a distinct pluralisation of politics, but did not particularly enhance state capacity: indeed, it was in 1972, during this "New Democracy" period, that Afghanistan experienced one of the worst famines in its history.

But the greatest weakness of the state lay in its fragile fiscal base. When Muhammad Zahir Shah ascended the throne, a substantial proportion of revenue was derived from taxes on land, and the vast bulk of state expenditure was covered by internal revenue sources. By the beginning of the democratic experiment in 1963, fully 49 per cent of state expenditure was covered by foreign aid.[13] This aid had funded a number of showcase developmental projects, but the general trend of dependence on so-called "rentier income" was very dangerous, since decisions beyond the control of the government could compromise the state's ability to fund its programs (and meet its promises to the Afghan people). This was exactly what happened from the late 1960s, and the result was growing popular dissatisfaction, and fertile ground for recruitment by radicals taking advantage of the pluralism of "New Democracy." The coups of 1973 and 1978 were disasters waiting to happen.

It is tempting to date the collapse of the state from the fall of the communist regime in April 1992, and indeed it was at this point that the army fractured along complex fault lines. But the better view is that the state effectively broke down at the end of the 1970s, around the time of the communist coup and the Soviet invasion. It encountered a crisis of both capacity and legitimacy. Between December 1979 and December 1991, a Soviet life-support system sustained the regimes of Babrak Karmal (1979–86) and Dr Najibullah (1986–92). The discontinuation of Soviet support – as a result of a Soviet–American agreement following the failed coup against Mikhail Gorbachev in August 1991 – led directly to the regime's collapse, as Najibullah lost access to the resources with which he had been buying the support of key notables in different parts of the country. The bulk of the countryside and the bulk of the population, however, lay beyond the writ of the central authorities throughout the 1980s. The practical consequence for Afghanistan at the turn of the twenty-first century is that the bulk of the population is relatively unfamiliar with the phenomenon of state power, and some stand to lose if the central state is effectively consolidated.

When significant state disruption occurs, the consequences will be felt quite swiftly in the sphere of security, for when military and police forces fragment, the state ceases to be in a position to provide a safe environment for ordinary people. Other mutual-support systems will come into play, ranging from local community-based gendarmeries to regional militias. Restoring a functioning security sector is one of the most difficult challenges of state-building, since at the outset ordinary people may be very reluctant to put their trust in new and untested state bodies. This can be so even if, in the abstract, they can recognise the importance of restoring the roles of the military and the police.

The erosion of trust

In recent years, considerable attention has been paid to the importance of trust as a feature of social relations. Much of this discussion has focused on developed western countries, and on the implications of a decline in citizens' willingness to trust their governments, which some observers see as alarming but others as a manifestation of healthy scepticism.[14] Rather less attention has been paid to the issue of trust in disrupted or war-torn societies, but it can credibly be argued that the effects of conflict on patterns of trust are among the most serious of its long-term consequences, and go a significant way towards explaining the difficulties that can arise in addressing the problems of a country like Afghanistan. A number of the features of such countries that outside observers find most perplexing – a compulsion to retain control of armaments, rampant nepotism and clientelism, and a resort to "identity politics" – can be seen as rational responses to a situation in which being too trusting can prove exceedingly dangerous.

According to one view, trust is grounded in expectations. As Barbara Misztal has put it, "to trust means to hold some expectations about something future or contingent or to have some belief as to how another person will perform on some future occasion. To trust is to believe that the results of somebody's intended action will be appropriate from our point of view."[15] But given that expectations can sometimes be disappointed, trusting someone or something carries an overtone of making oneself vulnerable. Trust, according to Charles Tilly, "consists of placing valued outcomes at risk to others' malfeasance, mistakes, or failures." He goes on to argue that trust relationships "include those in which people regularly take such risks," and defines trust networks as consisting of "ramified interpersonal connections, consisting mainly of strong ties, within which people set valued, consequential long-term resources and enterprises at risk to the malfeasance, mistakes, or failures of others."[16]

When the legitimacy and capacity of the state are significantly compromised, as was the case in Afghanistan, individuals will look to other support structures to sustain them. This is one reason why tribal loyalties can prove so potent in such situations: tribes are a form of mutual-support association, bound together by strong norms of reciprocity based on shared lineage.[17] But such networks are not neat building blocks for new political structures in a country in which such networks abound: weaving them elegantly together is an extremely daunting task, although Tilly is right to emphasise the fundamental importance of winning their support for the state. For example, the Taliban were drawn overwhelmingly from the Pushtun ethnic group, and relatively few Pushtuns took a strong stand against them; this is one factor accounting for some wariness towards Pushtuns among non-Pushtuns in the post-Taliban period. This is not to say that conflict has been primarily ethnic – it has not – but rather to note that in countries marked by high levels of social complexity, some wider civic commitments may be required if elite politics is to prove at all stable.[18]

Given Afghanistan's recent history, in which violence and terror have played prominent parts,[19] it is entirely rational for people to be suspicious of the aims and objectives of other individuals and groups. The costs of misplaced suspicion may be low for a given individual, whereas the costs of misplaced trust can be catastrophically high. To build civil politics, it is necessary to foster the re-establishment of trust, within the mass population but particularly at the level of political elites, since elite fragmentation is a notorious source of political instability. This is not an easy task, since trust relationships are a product ultimately of interactions over time: trust is built rather than created by decree. Nonetheless, there are several mechanisms that can be used to nurture trust. One, of possible value for the long run at the mass level, is *resocialisation*, using education to break down stereotypical ways of thinking. Another, of special importance for elite politics, is *institutional design*: different institutions create varying behavioural incentives, with some promoting more cooperative forms of behaviour than others. Perhaps of greatest importance in the short run is the establishment of a *neutral source of security*, to reduce the scale of risk associated with exposing valued outcomes to "the malfeasance, mistakes, or failures of others."[20]

The crystallisation of obstructive forces

One of the reasons why Afghanistan slid into disaster in the 1970s was that the political scene was increasingly populated with extremist groups with no particular commitment to the practice of politics in civil ways. These groups were strikingly teleological: they derived legitimacy in the eyes of their adherents not by reference to some democratic choice mechanism, but by reference to the end state they were committed to achieving. Where choice of political tactics was concerned, the desirability of the end justified the horror of the means adopted to pursue it. And while the leaders of a number of such groups may have been power-hungry cynics exploiting the gullibility of potential followers, they mobilised ideology very effectively to pursue their aims. One such ideology was Marxism-Leninism, still extremely popular in third world intellectual circles in the 1970s, and supported by an active Soviet propaganda apparatus and agents of the Soviet Committee of State Security, the KGB. In a country as poor as Afghanistan, it had a certain appeal among small-time intellectuals looking for simple explanations for the country's problems. Another ideology was radical Islamism, inspired by figures such as the Egyptian Sayid Qutb, who had been executed by the Egyptian government in 1966. The most notorious of these extremist groups was Hekmatyar's Hezb-e Islami.[21] The crisis of the Afghan state provided space for these groups to come to prominence even though they lacked any significant mass popular support. Hekmatyar's Hezb did not enjoy either strong regional or strong tribal backing, and abroad is now widely regarded as a terrorist group, but it remains a menace in various parts of Afghanistan.

The development of radical Islamist groups was facilitated by the forced displacement of millions of Afghans from their homes.

The "Refugee Tented Villages" set up in Pakistan by the Pakistan government became fertile territory for political activity, not least because Pakistan gave privileged positions in the camps to seven Afghan resistance parties, of which Hekmatyar's Hezb was one.[22] Moderate voices in the refugee population found themselves under threat, something highlighted by the murder in 1988, widely blamed on Hekmatyar,[23] of Sayid Bahauddin Majrooh, formerly a professor of philosophy at Kabul University, who had directed the respected Afghan Information Centre. Afghan refugee camps provided support for vast numbers of vulnerable, traumatised victims of conflict, but this was not all they did. The camps became recruiting grounds for combatants to resist the Soviet occupation of Afghanistan,[24] and were also exploited by radicals whose aim was not to resist the Soviets so much as to prepare for the struggle against moderate Muslims once the Soviet presence came to an end. In addition, the camps attracted the attention of radicals from other parts of the world, including Arabs from the Middle East and North Africa, and young Muslims from Southeast Asia.[25]

This set the scene for the emergence of the Taliban movement in 1994, as an alternative instrument of Pakistan's regional policy. In a real sense the young Taliban foot soldiers were themselves war victims, available for recruitment because of the extreme social dislocation the Soviet invasion had produced. Many were orphans from refugee camps who had never known any kind of "normal" life. The advent of the Taliban was received quite sentimentally in some western circles, where the naive belief that they would be a force for stability found voice.[26] US Assistant Secretary of State Robin Raphel responded to their occupation of Kabul in September 1996 by stating that "We have no quarrel with the Taliban in terms of their political legitimacy or lack thereof."[27] Not everyone was fooled: as Robert D. Blackwill, US ambassador to India from 2001 to 2003, later observed, "While we were looking at our shoelaces, New Delhi doggedly tried to warn us during these years that the Taliban were not exactly social reformers, but to no avail."[28] Although it was the gender policies of the Taliban that provoked the greatest international ire, their sustained brutality towards ethnic and sectarian minorities belied any claim that they had brought "peace": for the 2000 or more Afghans murdered by the Taliban in Mazar-e Sharif between 8 and 11 August 1998, the Taliban brought only the peace of the grave.[29] While Operation Enduring Freedom in 2001 obliterated the regime, it did not eliminate the Taliban altogether. Key figures, including Taliban leader Mullah Muhammad Omar, escaped capture, with many making their way to safety in Pakistan; and many ordinary Taliban also slipped across the border or melted away into remote communities in the south and east of Afghanistan.

The Taliban came to threaten the wider world as a result of their alliance with Osama Bin Laden's al-Qaeda. At one level, the two had less in common than a casual observer might have thought. Where the Taliban were determinedly anti-modernist, al-Qaeda was – like much radical Islamism – modernist in orientation[30] although virulently anti-western. But the Taliban were extremely useful to Bin Laden, providing him and his associates with an operational base, and the Taliban, in turn, were bound to Bin Laden both by obligations of hospitality, which figure strongly in Pushtun social codes, and by gratitude for support that Bin Laden had given them during their final thrust towards Kabul. In the months preceding the September 2001 attacks, the Taliban fell more and more under al-Qaeda's influence, and since Operation Enduring Freedom the two have been partners in seeking to attack Coalition forces and ordinary Afghans with a view to disrupting the transition that the overthrow of the Taliban regime began. Neither al-Qaeda nor the Taliban movement enjoys significant support from ordinary Afghans,[31] but even with a very narrow support base they are capable of acting as spoilers, attacking isolated targets and stirring up trouble for the government of Hamid Karzai and its external backers.

One other potentially obstructive force has received some discussion, and that is the phenomenon of the "warlord." The expression, popularised in discussions of China in the early twentieth century,[32] is a rather loose one. It came to be applied at different times to regional strongmen (such as Ismail Khan in

Herat), and to leaders of established armed formations (such as Muhammad Qasim Fahim, who took control of Ahmad Shah Massoud's forces after his assassination on 9 September 2001). It was particularly favoured as a pejorative expression by a number of Afghan émigrés who returned to take up executive positions in the post-Taliban administration after years of living abroad and then found themselves at odds over policy with former activists of the Mujahideen resistance to the Soviets and the Taliban.

"Warlord" can be a useful term to characterise militia leaders who survive overwhelmingly on the strength of their capacity to extract resources from an unwilling population and redistribute them to loyal commanders. But it is not particularly useful when attached to leaders – like Ismail Khan – who enjoy significant normative support.[33] Such figures, in contrast to the likes of Hekmatyar, were not committed to a strategy of "total spoiling." While some of them could exercise a degree of influence over ministry staff in Kabul,[34] and in the case of figures such as Abdul Rab al-Rasoul Sayyaf were quite extreme in their views,[35] they did not directly threaten Afghanistan's transition since they did not create space for total spoilers to operate. Far more dangerous have been the so-called "American warlords," who are mostly Taliban supporters who switched sides after 11 September 2001 and were rewarded by the Coalition for supplying intelligence about Taliban and al-Qaeda forces. Many received official positions in the post-Taliban era in their areas of ostensible military strength, contributing to significant problems of poor local governance; a number of them would readily switch their support to drug traffickers or the Taliban if offered a large enough bribe.

Regional meddling

A further challenge confronting Afghanistan relates to its regional position. Historically, Afghanistan functioned as a buffer state between the Russian Empire and British India, preventing direct confrontation between the two. This set the scene for a struggle for influence in Afghanistan, in which a number of states took part. Afghanistan was never exposed to colonial domination, but in the nineteenth century it twice found itself in direct conflict with the British, and it was only in 1919 after the Third Anglo–Afghan War that it secured full control over its foreign relations. That said, Afghanistan managed its foreign affairs with a considerable degree of dexterity. It remained neutral in both the First and Second World Wars, and during the Cold War adopted a formal position of non-alignment which, while increasingly compromised by aid flows in the 1950s from the Soviet Union, nonetheless remained the centrepiece of Afghanistan's foreign policy rhetoric.

Its regional relations, however, were significantly complicated from the late 1940s on. Within Afghanistan, some members of the Pushtun ethnic group had chafed at the 1893 demarcation of a boundary between Afghanistan and British India – the so-called "Durand Line" – which had divided the Pushtuns territorially. With the partition of India in 1947, they asserted that the Pushtuns of India should have had the opportunity to be reunited with their Afghan co-ethnics. As a result, Afghanistan voted against the admission of the new state of Pakistan to the United Nations, and in the years that followed Afghanistan was paradoxically much closer to the Hindu-majority state of India than to the Muslim-majority state of Pakistan. Indeed, the "Pushtunistan dispute" had a poisonous effect on Afghanistan–Pakistan relations, and even led to the severing of diplomatic relations between 1961 and 1963. The consequence was that successive Pakistani leaderships were extremely fearful of Afghan nationalism. The military regime of General Zia ul-Haq (1977–88), committed in any case to a policy of Islamisation, felt much more comfortable supporting Islamic radicals such as Hekmatyar's Hezb, since such figures seemed less likely to revive a territorial dispute based on tribal and ethnic identifications. Pakistan's long-term strategy from the time of the Soviet invasion was therefore to identify and promote pliable Afghan clients of Islamic rather than nationalist disposition. The principal agency involved was the Inter-Services Intelligence Directorate of the Pakistan armed forces, or ISI, and the principal Afghan clients were first Hekmatyar and then, once his inadequacies had been exposed, the Taliban.[36] The ease with which the Taliban continue to operate out of Pakistan suggests that Pakistan's long-term strategy remains in place, and this is a matter of very serious concern for the Karzai government.

Afghanistan's regional challenges go beyond those posed by Pakistan. Iran, to the west, also has interests in Afghanistan. A Shiite-majority state, Iran has long had a sense of protective responsibility towards Afghanistan's Shiite minority. Its relations with the Taliban were poor, and war between Iran and the Taliban nearly broke out in August 1998 when Pakistani extremists who formed part of the Taliban force that massacred thousands of civilians in Mazar-e Sharif also murdered staff of the Iranian consulate. Although Operation Enduring Freedom brought large numbers of US troops close to the Iranian border, Iran has hitherto played a constructive role in post-Taliban Afghanistan. Should the hostility between the United States and Iran take yet another sharp turn for the worse, however, Iran would be well placed to stir up trouble for the United States not only in Iraq but in Afghanistan as well. Iran, in contrast to Pakistan, has no aspiration to dominate Afghanistan, but it is keen to see that Afghanistan not be used as a springboard for challenges to key Iranian interests.

Afghanistan is also entangled in the wider question of the future shape of greater Central Asia, and developments to its north have implications for its stability. After the Soviet leadership achieved control over much of Central Asia through the suppression of the Basmachi movement in the 1920s and 1930s, the region was for decades a relatively quiet one. But the disintegration of the Soviet Union at the end of 1991 created a complex new geopolitical landscape. The new rulers of Kazakhstan, Uzbekistan, Turkmenistan, Tajikistan, and Kyrgyzstan deployed a range of stratagems to legitimate their exercise of power, and sought to build links with other regional states and more remote powers. During the Taliban period, Afghanistan was inadvertently drawn into this cauldron, as energy companies such as the US corporation UNOCAL and the Argentinian company Bridas competed for the opportunity to construct gas pipelines from

Turkmenistan through Afghanistan to markets in South Asia.[37] More recently, Central Asia has re-emerged as a venue for regional competition, of sorts, between the United States, China, and the Russian Federation, not least because the American use of an air base in Uzbekistan as part of its "war on terror" led some to fear a concerted US push for long-term influence in the region.[38] At some point, there is a risk that Afghanistan too might become a venue for such competition, although not until the danger of the recrudescence of al-Qaeda has passed.

Finally, Afghanistan's situation cannot be divorced from the wider strategic context in the Middle East created by the US invasion of Iraq in 2003. The ferocity of the opposition to intervention has alarming implications for fragile states such as Afghanistan, since the transnational radical forces conjured into action by the invasion have the ability to affect other parts of the world as well. This is not only by virtue of the movement of personnel from one theatre of operations to another, but also through the spread of particular kinds of terror tactics. Thus far, the attacks on US forces in Iraq and on ordinary Iraqis whom the United States and its political allies are unable to protect have been on a scale much greater than in Afghanistan, and Kabul is nowhere near as insecure as Baghdad. This could, however, change. Simply in terms of person-to-person connections, Afghanistan is now more densely integrated with the wider world than ever before. Planes fly regularly between Kabul and the Gulf, and Dubai in the United Arab Emirates is now one of the largest Pushto-speaking cities in the region. Those leaders crafting policy for diverse parts of the Middle East would do well to bear in mind the possible implications of their actions for stability in Afghanistan.

The risk of abandonment

Afghanistan has historically received international attention for all the wrong reasons. States that have engaged with Afghanistan have typically done so not out of concern for the well-being of the Afghan people, but in defence of interests of their own. Perhaps there is not much surprising in this, but the consequence has been that western engagement with Afghanistan has been fitful, rather than durable and systematic. And such fitful engagement has consequences of its own, most notably for the confidence of Afghans that times have finally changed.

The 1950s saw a degree of competition between the United States and the Soviet Union for influence in Afghanistan, but the United States ultimately proved to be less than a serious competitor, since it was more interested in building relations with Pakistan as a key "northern tier" state. In the 1960s and 1970s, the United States and Afghanistan maintained civil relations, but with no particular degree of intimacy. The violent death of US Ambassador Adolph Dubs in February 1979 in Kabul led to the downgrading of US–Afghan relations, and in early 1989 the US embassy was closed down completely, and remained closed until after the Taliban were ousted. Through the 1980s, the main US involvement in Afghanistan came in the form of support for the Mujahideen. This aid was substantial, and in principle well justified: the Soviet invasion of Afghanistan constituted an egregious violation of the Charter of the United Nations. But the means by which the aid was provided left a lot to be desired. As Ambassador Robert D. Blackwill put it in 2005, "the United States in effect subcontracted its Afghan policy in the past to Pakistan's intelligence service, which in turn fostered the growth of Islamic zealotry across the border in Afghanistan and with it, the rise of the Taliban."[39] The consequences for moderate Afghan nationalists of Pakistan's intermediation were severe, and the forces of Ahmad Shah Massoud were especially disadvantaged. As Olivier Roy has recorded, from November 1988 until October 1990, Massoud "did not receive a single bullet from the US-sponsored programme."[40]

Despite what is sometimes claimed, there is no evidence of US assistance during the 1980s to Osama Bin Laden, but what actually happened was bad enough, at least from the viewpoint of moderate Afghans. Some US officials were far too readily influenced by self-interested Pakistani interlocutors, to the deep frustration of those US representatives who could see what Pakistan's Inter-Services

Intelligence Directorate was out to achieve.[41] One would hope that the lessons of this experience have been properly absorbed by those in western capitals with responsibility for the running of covert operations.

What particularly seared the consciousness of Afghan political actors was the haste with which the United States walked away from them once the Soviet leadership moved to withdraw its troops from Afghanistan. This did not reflect a deliberate decision to "abandon" the Mujahideen, but rather a preoccupation with events elsewhere, particularly in the Soviet Union itself where Soviet leader Mikhail Gorbachev was attempting to maintain his dominance in the face of mounting right-wing opposition. The administration of President George H. W. Bush was extremely reluctant to add to Gorbachev's difficulties, either in Afghanistan or in other flashpoints such as the Baltic states. Nonetheless, from the Afghans' point of view, America as an ally was no longer what it had once been.[42] This situation proved even more acute after the collapse of the communist regime in April 1992. The United States did not re-open its Kabul embassy, as one might have expected it to, and very little aid flowed to the new Afghan regime, headed first by Sebghatullah Mojadiddi and then from June 1992 by Burhanuddin Rabbani.

If anything, the situation for Afghan moderates actually deteriorated during the Clinton administration (1993–2001). While the administration's flirtation with the Taliban was relatively short-lived and no credible evidence ever surfaced that Washington had supported the Taliban directly, it was very slow to recognise the threat that was taking shape. According to a Congressional Research Service report, Clinton administration officials stated that "they did not take major action to oust the Taliban from power, either through direct U.S. military action or by providing military aid to Taliban opponents, because domestic U.S. support for those steps was then lacking and because the Taliban's opponents were considered too weak and not consistent with U.S. values."[43] This reluctance to associate with the Taliban's opponents may have derived from a misguided concern for Pakistani sensitivities, but one very experienced observer rightly described it as a display of "staggering negligence, or myopia."[44]

The reason that these experiences of past neglect are important is that they account for what might seem a certain obstreperousness on the part of Afghan political actors. When anti-Taliban forces occupied Kabul from the north of the city against American wishes in November 2001, they did so partly because they did not trust US judgement in putting together a new political dispensation for the country. When the United States urges the Karzai government not to criticise Pakistan over ongoing Taliban raids into Afghanistan, Afghan officials remember the US's naive toleration of Pakistan's promotion of Hekmatyar and then the Taliban. The Afghans find themselves in a very difficult situation. Given the ongoing threat posed by the Taliban, they need outside support; but they need supporters more attuned to the realities of their situation than the United States has historically proved to be. Maintaining the right kind of international support is one of the most burdensome challenges that Afghanistan faces.

This account of Afghanistan's problems is necessarily very brief, but it highlights how important it is for Afghanistan to succeed in reconstituting the political system, rebuilding security, promoting human development, and managing relations with the wider world. These issues are the subject of the next four chapters.

CHAPTER 2

Reconstituting the political system

One consequence of Afghanistan's decades of disruption is a great deal of popular cynicism about what politics can deliver. Nonetheless, the task of reconstituting the political system is central to the promotion of long-term stability. A challenge for the architects of change has been to accomplish this goal in such a way that cynicism is gradually replaced by confidence in the future. Given recent history, this is a very large challenge indeed.

The overthrow of the Taliban created an immediate need for new political arrangements. While the "Islamic State of Afghanistan" headed by Burhanuddin Rabbani occupied Afghanistan's seat in the UN General Assembly, it commanded no functioning agencies or instrumentalities; and although forces associated with the old Islamic State had occupied Kabul on 13 November 2001, not even Rabbani argued that it could simply resume its old position. It was widely recognised, and accepted, that a process was required through which new state structures could be designed and a new political leadership constituted and legitimated. Fortunately, the United Nations was on hand to help with this process, and in the special representative of the secretary-general, Lakhdar Brahimi, it had a guardian of uncommon sensitivity who was able to listen carefully to the claims of different Afghan political actors. With the support of the German government, Brahimi convened a meeting in Bonn from 27 November to 5 December 2001 that brought together a range of non-Taliban Afghan political actors with officials of the United Nations, representatives of a number of governments, and expert consultants. There were some notable absences, including President Rabbani, former King Zahir, the future President Hamid Karzai, and the Uzbek strongman Abdul Rashid Dostam. Nor were the proceedings without their drama: the Pushtun Haji Abdul Qadir and the Hazara Muhammad Karim Khalili left in protest at what they saw as insufficient attention to their demands. Nonetheless, the proceedings were marked by a high sense of purpose; and some participants, such as Massoud's former aide Younos Qanuni, shone in the small group format, acting as bridge-builders between different interests. These factors contributed to the development of a creative and imaginative map for political reconstruction.

Crafting a transitional path: capacity and legitimacy

The Bonn conference laid out a path for political transition in Afghanistan. The negotiations concluded with the adoption on 5 December of an "Agreement on Provisional Arrangements in Afghanistan Pending the Re-establishment of Permanent Government Institutions," consisting of a principal text and three annexes, which was endorsed the following day by the UN Security Council in Resolution 1383. The agreement stipulated that "An Interim Authority shall be established upon the official transfer of power on 22 December 2001," to consist of "an Interim Administration presided over by a Chairman, a Special Independent Commission for the Convening of the Emergency Loya Jirga [Great Assembly], and a Supreme Court of Afghanistan, as well as such other courts as may be established by the Interim Administration." It provided that "An Emergency Loya Jirga shall be convened within six months of the establishment of the Interim Authority. The Emergency Loya Jirga will be opened by His Majesty Mohammed Zaher, the former King of Afghanistan. The Emergency Loya Jirga shall decide on a Transitional Authority, including a broad-based transitional administration, to lead Afghanistan until such time as a fully representative government can be elected through free and fair elections to be held no later than two years from the date of the convening of the Emergency Loya Jirga." It also provided that "A Constitutional Loya Jirga shall be convened within eighteen months of the establishment of the Transitional Authority, in order to adopt a new constitution for Afghanistan."

The agreement went on to depict the shape of the interim administration, which was to be "composed of a Chairman, five Vice Chairmen and 24 other members. Each member, except the Chairman, may head a department of the Interim Administration." The interim administration was to be "entrusted with the day-to-day conduct of the affairs of state," and had "the right to issue decrees for the peace, order and good government of Afghanistan." The agreement also stated that "the Interim Administration shall have full jurisdiction over the printing and delivery of the national currency and special drawing rights from international financial institutions. The Interim Administration shall establish, with the assistance of the United Nations, a Central Bank of Afghanistan that will regulate the money supply of the country through transparent and accountable procedures." Finally, the agreement made provision for two commissions: an "independent Civil Service Commission to provide the Interim Authority and the future Transitional Authority with shortlists of candidates for key posts in the administrative departments, as well as those of governors and *uluswals*, in order to ensure their competence and integrity"; and an "independent Human Rights Commission, whose responsibilities will include human rights monitoring, investigation of violations of human rights, and development of domestic human rights institutions."

The Bonn approach was premised on the recognition that the re-establishment of state capacity would be a slow and laborious process, and that no single strategy of political legitimation would be effective for the entire Afghan population. Thus it envisaged a model in which different approaches would be used to elicit the support of different elements of the population, thereby building layers of legitimacy around a new system of rule. The key approaches involved weaving together traditional strategies (based on the authority and reputation of the former king and the idea of the Loya Jirga, a quintessentially Pushtun institution), charismatic strategies (based on the attractive personality of Hamid Karzai, a long-time resistance notable who emerged as a consensus candidate to head the interim administration), and legal–rational strategies (based on the eventual holding of free and fair elections). The Bonn participants, and the United Nations more generally, realised that these would only work if the interim and then the transitional administrations could be seen to be making concrete differences in the lives of ordinary people, but this lay beyond the capacity of the Bonn meeting to ordain by decree. Not everyone accepted the logic of the Bonn approach. One American writer has recently put forward the outlandish claim that "the international community… believed that the main and essential measure needed to establish legitimacy was the holding of national elections." In fact, the United Nations emphasised the importance of a much more nuanced approach, and was cautious about according electoral processes a central position. The same writer goes on to claim that the participants at Bonn "sacrificed the legitimacy of their new construct to what they wrongly conceived as the higher value of sovereignty," and that 2003–04 witnessed a "breakthrough for legitimacy" through the restoration of "balances within the government."[1] This entire argument is radically misconceived, reflects a failure to appreciate the subtlety of Brahimi's approach, and cannot readily explain why, if there was such a "breakthrough," the Karzai government is increasingly beleaguered in the very areas whose inhabitants should have been appeased by the alleged restoration of "balances."[2] The Bonn conference *of course* could not produce instant legitimacy for a new administration, and it is fanciful to suppose that this was within its capacity. But the Bonn participants did *not* lose sight of the importance of legitimacy, and their endeavours constituted a significant step forward.[3]

The choice of the 44-year-old Hamid Karzai as chairman of the interim administration was also a positive move. All in all, it is difficult to see who – from the available candidates – could have done better than Karzai in what was an extremely difficult job. He was not initially the frontrunner to chair the interim administration;

nor was he a puppet of the United States. He was well known to most Afghan party activists from the 1980s, having served as Mojadiddi's spokesman in Peshawar, and then briefly as deputy foreign minister after the fall of the communist regime. He came from a moderate Pushtun family and his father, a prominent figure from the royalist period, had been assassinated in Quetta in July 1999 in a slaying widely interpreted as a Taliban warning to moderates not to oppose them. Despite this, Karzai remained an outspoken critic of the Taliban.[4] He was also widely respected for his personal decency, and displayed none of the ethnic chauvinism that some Afghan politicians had on occasion manifested. These talents made him an effective leader for the early transition, and an outstandingly impressive public face of Afghanistan to the wider world.

But Karzai also had a number of weaknesses. One related to his ability to run an efficient personal office. While he had some excellent staff, he had some very ineffective associates as well, and years into his tenure the operations of his office remained chaotic, with too much power in the hands of individuals with stronger ethnic agendas than he had. A second problem related to security. On 6 July 2002, Karzai's vice-president Haji Abdul Qadir was assassinated in broad daylight in downtown Kabul. After Karzai himself survived an assassination attempt in Kandahar on 5 September 2002 he curtailed his travel; for some years, he was surrounded by American bodyguards from the DynCorp firm, which prompted strong criticism from ordinary Afghans.[5] A third problem for Karzai related to his political style. Karzai was very much a product of the state-free "Peshawar" politics in which he was schooled in exile in the 1980s – a politics based on networking, patronage, and the construction of prudential alliances. Detailed policy-making was not his strength, and this became a problem once the adoption of a strong presidential constitution thrust into his hands the responsibility for policy leadership. In the eyes of some, he became overly dependent for policy advice on the Afghan-born US ambassador from 2003 to 2005, Dr Zalmay Khalilzad, who had strong views of his own on what "nation-building" required.[6] Karzai's fourth weakness derived from his inclination to pacify potential troublemakers (in both

Kabul and beyond) by offering them positions in the state, which naturally annoyed those who argued that disloyalty was attracting rewards and that Karzai had devalued competence as a criterion for advancement. An insidious – although not widely publicised – consequence of all this has been that elite politics has been marked by ferocious rivalries, competition for the president's attention and favour, and denigration of opponents as a way of reducing their influence. As a result, some very gifted Afghans have left government positions in Kabul, disillusioned by the malice, backbiting, and spite they encountered. Beyond Kabul, the results have been even more destructive. It cannot be said too often that awarding offices to undeserving figures at provincial and local levels is a recipe for dramatically poor governance and the progressive erosion of the legitimacy of the state.

Karzai's relationship with the United States and Khalilzad was a source of both strength and weakness. On the one hand, since none of the Bonn parties wanted to see the United States walk away from Afghanistan a second time, Karzai's position as a US favourite worked to his advantage at the elite level. On the other hand, his apparent dependence on US backing led to hostile whispering. This was particularly so during the Emergency Loya Jirga from 11 to 19 June 2002, when Khalilzad moved forcefully to head off a push amongst delegates to promote Zahir Shah. At one level, the American intervention was a commonsense one – at 87 years of age, the former king was in no position to provide dynamic leadership, and his elevation would have set the scene for fierce political struggle once he died – but the way in which Khalilzad acted struck many observers as tactless, not least because it made Karzai look puny. This incident also coincided with a flexing of muscle by Defence Minister Muhammad Qasim Fahim, whose associates threw their weight around quite blatantly, leading many delegates to feel marginalised and frustrated when they should have been feeling empowered.

While the Bonn agreement contained much aspirational rhetoric that was remote from the drab and squalid realities of daily life in most parts of Afghanistan,[7] the process by which it was

35

devised demonstrated the truth of an old maxim that politics is the art of the possible. Two of the most insightful critics of post-Bonn developments, Chris Johnson and Jolyon Leslie, label it "the best deal that could be obtained at the time."[8] Pakistan and some Americans with Orientalist tendencies may have clung to the belief that it would be possible to marginalise the anti-Taliban forces drawn from non-Pushtun groups and establish a pro-Pakistan regime, but this was never a realistic possibility.[9] Those who had spent years battling the Taliban and their Pakistani backers were in no mood to see Pakistan re-establish a presence by back-door means, and for this reason the anti-Taliban forces were insistent on controlling what some saw as the heartland of power, namely the defence and interior ministries, which were allocated to Muhammad Qasim Fahim and Younos Qanuni. Yet those who saw this as simply handing over state power to a narrow faction missed two key points.

One was that with politics shifting in the direction of state-building, political power would come not just from the barrel of a gun but from the ability to mobilise human and financial resources. This made for more complex post-Bonn politics than many had expected. The other was that the anti-Taliban forces were not a unified collective, but rather a loose network of actors with the potential to split from each other as new political issues and opportunities arose. While post-Bonn elite conflict was sometimes painted as reflecting a "Pushtun–Panjsheri" schism (the latter name deriving from Ahmad Shah Massoud's native Panjsher valley), the reality was more complicated, and involved division along three distinct lines, although with significant overlap between them. Certainly some Pushtuns, mindful of past Pushtun domination of the national political elite and alarmed by anti-Pushtun pogroms in northern Afghanistan in the wake of the Taliban's removal, felt resentful of power exercised by some leaders of Panjsheri Tajik background, most importantly Fahim. But Fahim was also regarded with suspicion by some of Massoud's closest associates, which points to the dangers of depicting elite rivalry as a simple Pushtun–Panjsheri struggle.

Two other lines of division were important as well. One was a division on ideological lines, between Islamists who favoured some kind of explicitly "Islamic" state (however defined) and Muslims who were wary of Islamic activists as political actors and favoured a state based on public law rather than Islamic law as interpreted by conservative Islamic jurists. The other division, between former Mujahideen and Afghan expatriates, was particularly serious. After June 2002 Karzai's administration included a number of very gifted expatriates who had skills that were vital to postwar reconstruction and state-building programs, and whose claim to exercise power was grounded in their expertise. On the other hand, there were also ministers in the cabinet who had less administrative experience but mounted a claim to power on the basis of their steadfast opposition – as Mujahideen – first to the Soviet Union and then to the Taliban, in circumstances that were frequently dangerous and unpleasant, and at times when their expatriate adversaries were living comfortably in the west. Some of these Mujahideen were particularly scornful of Pushtun expatriates whom they regarded as having been less-than-vociferous critics of Taliban extremism.

It was the shifting nature of these political alliances that accounted for Fahim's increasing marginalisation. Dropped as Karzai's vice-presidential running mate on 26 July 2004,[10] he was replaced as defence minister by Abdul Rahim Wardak five months later – although in a mark of the fluidity of the situation, this cabinet reshuffle also witnessed the replacement of finance minister Ashraf Ghani, a Taliban critic who had enjoyed wide support from the donor community.

The design of the state

Given the reality of state collapse in Afghanistan, the Bonn agenda of reconstituting the state as an immediate focus of activity was both obvious and sensible.[11] "The state," however, is a more complex idea than is often appreciated. Joel S. Migdal has usefully distinguished four elements of any functioning state. First are the *trenches*, consisting of "the officials who must execute state directives directly in the face of possibly strong societal resistance." Second are the *dispersed field offices*, the "regional and local bodies that rework and organize state policies and directives for local consumption, or even formulate and implement wholly local policies." Third are the *agency's central offices*, the "nerve centers where national policies are formulated and enacted and where resources for implementation are marshaled." And fourth are the *commanding heights*, the "pinnacle of the state" where the "top executive leadership" is to be found.[12] A practical challenge in state-building is that it is performance at the lower levels that most affects the way a new state is viewed, yet it is the upper echelons that tend to attract immediate attention, not least because it is from there that decrees and instructions to the lower levels need to originate. In Afghanistan, the upper levels indeed received the earliest attention, with the consequence that regional power-holders stamped their control over certain state functions at the local level. This resulted in a rift between the formal (*de jure*) and functioning (*de facto*) states.[13]

The Bonn agreement provision that each member of the interim administration could head a department proved an unfortunate one. Instead of the reconstruction of the state beginning with a careful examination of what the state should be responsible for doing, of what its scope and strength should be,[14] it began with an apportionment of offices premised on the view that what the state should be doing had already been established. Public offices were thus treated as positional goods to be distributed as rewards for political loyalty rather than as repositories of public trust. The consequence was that many ministries became political fiefdoms for different political forces rather than embryonic components of an integrated whole. Furthermore, the proliferation of ministries created significant overlap between ministerial functions, setting the scene for dysfunctional turf battles: a government containing separate ministries of finance, commerce, planning, reconstruction, public works, rural reconstruction and development, and agriculture was a government poised for turmoil. Dr Ashraf Ghani, a former World Bank official who served as finance minister from

June 2002 until his replacement in December 2004, succeeded in imposing a degree of coherence by dint of his vision and forceful personality, but the institutional obstacles to coherent policy-making remained considerable. The casual, politically motivated adoption of an agency structure that bore little rational relation to Afghanistan's needs at the beginning of the twenty-first century was – to put it mildly – regrettable.

While Afghanistan has on paper a highly centralised, unitary system of government, in practice the exercise of state power is complicated by the existence of a system of provinces and provincial governors. There are currently 34 provinces, with the two newest, Panjsher and Dai Kundi, having been created by presidential decree after 2001. Within the provinces there are over 350 districts and over 200 municipalities, but there is considerable uncertainty as to their exact boundaries. The degree of effective local power is considerable. A 2005 World Bank study concluded that "in the revenue-rich provinces, governors make resource allocation decisions except on basic salaries. Staff appointments from Kabul are often rejected in favor of those loyal to regional factions, and even Kabul-based appointments often reflect loyalties and ethnic ties rather than merit. In these areas, where the warlords (and in some cases governors) have 'captured' both strategic decision-making and overall fiscal resources, the public sector is essentially autonomous from the central government."[15]

Provincial governors are centrally appointed, but often for political reasons rather than as a tribute to merit. The most egregious example has been Gul Agha Sherzai in Kandahar. Gul Agha is the son of a renowned Mujahideen commander, Haji Abdul Latif, who was poisoned in mysterious circumstances on 7 August 1989. He was nominally the governor of Kandahar at the time of the Taliban assault in 1994, although he fled before they arrived. He was restored to the position by Karzai, but proved such an embarrassment, not least because of his friendly relations with drug barons, that he was brought to Kabul as urban development minister, a position for which experts engaging with him found him completely unequipped. In December 2004, he was removed as minister but restored to his earlier position as governor of Kandahar. It was hardly surprising that Kandahar remained one of the least stable provinces in the country, and eventually Gul Agha was replaced, but not before he had done a great deal of harm. The contrast between him and Ismail Khan was striking. Ismail, in Herat, ran a strict but efficient regime, based partly on customs revenues collected at the border with Iran and only partially remitted to Kabul. Under pressure from the United States, and following the death of his son in a militia attack, he relinquished his position in Herat in 2004 and became the power and energy minister in Kabul. According to several accounts, both security and administrative efficiency deteriorated markedly after Ismail's departure.

One of the most surprising features of administration in Afghanistan has been the survival of local administrative structures in at least skeletal form throughout the years of bitter internal struggle.[16] They may have survived simply because nominal occupation of a state position, even on an unpaid basis, was a source of some social status. But this does not mean that the local state structures will remain intact in the face of changing circumstances. As new actors, both governmental and non-governmental, position themselves to perform reconstruction tasks in the various districts of the country, opportunities will emerge for old state employees to obtain better-remunerated work. There is thus a risk that outlying components of the state will fall victim to a kind of internal "brain drain."

Civil society and participation

Drawing on the strength of "civil society" was one of the objectives of those who arranged the Bonn meeting. During his tenure as special representative of the UN secretary-general from 1997 to 1999, Lakhdar Brahimi had consulted widely with different Afghan groups, listening to their arguments and noting their concerns. He was fully aware that those who took part in the formal meeting at Bonn represented relatively narrow strata of society and opinion, and was determined to ensure that other perspectives could also be injected into the discussions. To meet this need, an "Afghan Civil Society Meeting" was run in parallel with the Bonn meeting, with ideas from the former injected into the discussions at the latter. As a consequence, "civil society" came to be seen as a force whose meaningful participation was vital to the transition. This has had mixed effects, some clearly positive, some less so.

"Civil society" is historically a European expression. It emerged as commercial and industrial agents were assuming more complex forms, especially through the formation of guilds. The German expression *bürgerliche Gesellschaft*, which preceded the modern expression *Zivilgesellschaft*, captured this rather neatly. The term "civil society" came over time to characterise forms of social organisation that enjoy a reasonable degree of autonomy from the command structures of the state. But "civil society" is not an actor as such. In western countries, organised collectives of market actors form an important element of civil society, as do civic associations of diverse kinds.[17] It is a mistake to assume that analogous agents are to be found in significant numbers in Afghanistan. The components of "civil society" in the western sense operate within a framework of rules that define particular forms of organisation (such as corporations, registered societies, and unincorporated associations). In Afghanistan, the disintegration of the state involved the breakdown of any such framework, although indigenous non-government organisations and councils (*shuras*) to some extent filled the vacuum. There are distinctive forms of relationship based on affinity and reciprocity which are captured by the word *qawm*. The word is difficult to translate, but "network" comes close. Networks, of course, are difficult to incorporate into decision-making processes, for they are relational rather than hierarchical, and not "actors" in any strong sense of the term.

Furthermore, not all components of "society" are "civil." There are good reasons to be wary of some of the groups that may operate or take shape in Afghanistan during the transition process. The most obvious groups to watch are those that might seek to mobilise around claims of ethnic superiority. There is also a risk that groups claiming to speak for historically marginalised elements of the population will be composed of extremists rather than mainstream elements. Finally, it is important to recognise that not all legitimate interests will be articulated by groups which crystallise to express them. The logic of collective action implies that the scale of bene-fit to individual beneficiaries will shape the ways in which interests are organisationally expressed.[18] Thus, some legitimate interests (those that significantly benefit a small number of people) may be more strongly defended than other legitimate interests (those that modestly benefit a large number of people). Furthermore, the articulate beneficiaries of privileges under past regimes may be better placed to voice their concerns than the downtrodden. It is important that attempts to provide space for "civil society" not simply empower groups that for historical reasons are better placed to organise themselves.

Despite all these qualifications, a number of the initiatives undertaken to empower "civil society" have been beneficial. Fol-lowing the contribution made by the Afghan Civil Society Meeting, consultation with "civil society" groups was institution-alised through the establishment of the Afghan Civil Society Forum, supported by the Swiss Peace Foundation.[19] The forum staff were alert to the diversity of "civil society" and also to the existence of different strata within social groups that might appear obvious candidates for assistance, such as women and various ethnic minorities. Nor did they crudely equate "civil society" with non-government organisations, which are a part – but only a part – of civil society, broadly interpreted. That said, however, it is important to recognise that Afghans live simultaneously in many different social worlds, and the more formalised attempts to engage with them will be necessarily limited in what they can accomplish.

The principal instrument to link the state and "civil society" has been a set of initiatives known as the National Solidarity Program, based on the idea of community-driven development. Its key ele-ments are facilitation of local decision-making and priority setting; block grants (of up to US$60,000) for activities of elected Community Development Councils; capacity-building for council members; and strengthening of institutional linkages.[20] The promise held out by the program was high: "community grants," according to two extremely well-informed observers, Nicholas Leader and Mohammed Haneef Atmar, "will put decision-making in the hands of communities, enable the state to bypass warlord structures to provide resources to communities directly, and promote the development of community-level democracy and decision-making as the basis for a more democratic polity."[21] While early signs are positive, the jury is still out on what long-term effects the National Solidarity Program will have, and whether it will prove sustainable.[22] Certain types of projects require a mix of capital and recurrent funding if they are to succeed: schooling is an obvious example. Furthermore, a sudden inflow of resources can create a "stake" over which locals then battle, and Chris Johnson and Jolyon Leslie have warned that the scheme "risks becoming a donor-funded version of the old system of patronage, rather than a genuine mechanism for participation."[23] Finally, the National Solidarity Program is essentially a rural development program, without a direct urban analogue.

Drafting a new constitution

While the Bonn agreement was concerned with tracing out a path for state-building, it did not directly address the question of how the "commanding heights" of the state were to be structured. Instead, it ordained the continuation of most of Afghanistan's 1964 constitution until a Constitutional Loya Jirga devised and adopted a replacement text. This agenda culminated in the Loya Jirga held between 14 December 2003 and 4 January 2004 and the adoption of the new constitution (*Qanun-e Asasi-i Afghanistan*). The Constitutional Loya Jirga had 502 members, most of them elected through an indirect but lively process and some of them appointed by Karzai.

The term "constitution" is an ancient one,[24] but its meaning is not always well understood. A country's constitution, whether codified or uncodified, is best seen as its fundamental law, identifying the actors and institutions that craft, execute and interpret laws, and defining the limits of their powers. Constitutions are important at a symbolic level, which is why even totalitarian states have on occasion adopted ostensibly liberal constitutions – witness the meaningless Soviet constitution of 1936 – to create the impression that they are not as grim as they seem. But constitutions are also important as a source of order. The challenge for their makers is to devise a constitution that will prevent power from being so concentrated that it facilitates dictatorial government, while also preventing power from being so fragmented that it leads to ineffectual and unworkable government.[25] If a constitution takes root, it can stabilise relations between hitherto hostile elites by providing rules that ensure political contestation occurs in a courteous fashion. While many constitutions have been largely for show, well-crafted, widely accepted constitutions can contribute mightily to a change in political atmosphere. But new constitutions must pass from infancy through adolescence to adulthood, and in their early years remain vulnerable to attack. Thus, we cannot be certain just how significant the constitution-drafting exercise of 2003–04 will ultimately prove to have been.

The drafting process was complex. A commission of nine drafted the initial text, which was then vetted by a Constitutional Commission of 35 and by the National Security Council. While members of the commission were supplied with detailed briefings (translated into Persian and Pushto) from international experts on institutional design, the final product reflected more the insistence of Karzai that the text incorporate a strong presidential system.[26] While "public consultation" sessions were mounted, they actually preceded the release of the draft constitution on 3 November 2003, which gave them a somewhat surreal quality. The Constitutional Loya Jirga itself, chaired by Sebghatullah Mojadiddi, ran more smoothly than the chaotic Emergency Loya Jirga, although it too had its stormy moments, such as Mojadiddi's attempt to eject a female delegate who seized the opportunity to attack radical Mujahideen.[27] The weakness of the Loya Jirga was one endemic to such exercises: much of the key politicking took place in private meetings, out of the public gaze, blunting the claim that the process was transparent and accountable.

The 2004 constitution, adopted after fierce debate at the Constitutional Loya Jirga, has notable strengths, but potentially significant flaws as well.[28] It provides for a president (*Rais-e Jamhur*) and two vice-presidents (Article 60), with the president to be elected by the French system (that is, a first round of voting, which, if no candidate receives more than 50 per cent of the votes, is to be followed two weeks later by a run-off poll between the two candidates with the largest number of votes). The president is limited to two five-year terms (Article 61). The powers of the president, set out in Article 64, include determining "the fundamental policies of the country (*keshwar*) with the approval of the National Assembly (*Shura-i Milli*)," serving as Commander-in-Chief, and appointing ministers, the head of the Central Bank, and the head and members of the Supreme Court "with the endorsement of the Wolesi Jirga." Article 72 requires that ministers have "higher education," and "exclusive citizenship of Afghanistan." The National Assembly, under Article 82, is a bicameral legislature consisting of the House of the People (*Wolesi Jirga*) and House of Elders (*Meshrano Jirga*). Members of the Wolesi Jirga serve five-year terms. The National Assembly under Article 90 has the power of "ratification (*taswib*), modification or abrogation of laws and/or legislative decrees," and can adopt a vote of no confidence in a minister.

According to Article 94, "Law is what both houses of the National Assembly approve and the president endorses, unless this Constitution states otherwise." Yet Article 121 provides that the Supreme Court, on the request "of the Government or the courts," can "review laws, legislative decrees, and conventions on their compliance with the Constitution and their interpretation, in accordance with the law." This is a striking provision, for while Article 7 provides that the state "shall observe the United Nations Charter, international treaties and conventions that Afghanistan has ratified, and the Universal Declaration of Human Rights," Article 3 provides that in Afghanistan no law shall contravene the "beliefs and provisions" (*motaqidat wa ahkam*) of the sacred religion of

Islam. This last provision represents a notable departure from the wording of Article 64 of the 1964 constitution, which referred to the more limited notion of "basic principles" (*asasat*).[29] This has the potential to deliver considerable power to unelected and very conservative jurists linked to Abdul Rab al-Rasoul Sayyaf.[30]

While the process of securing a new constitution was widely hailed as a success, it did have its weaknesses. One related to the way in which endorsement of a strong presidential system was secured. This was a key demand of some Pushtun activists, and was vigorously promoted by Karzai's lobbying team at the Loya Jirga, but the result was a severe aggravation of ethnic tensions, especially when Karzai's unelected appointees proved a decisive bloc.[31] And this procedural problem was related to a wider substantive one. Presidential systems come in diverse forms,[32] but can be a recipe for disaster where societies or political elites are deeply divided: a pure presidential system effectively permits only one winner,[33] while potentially generating many disgruntled losers. Karzai's non-confrontational personality may have hidden this problem for the moment, but it is lying buried just below the surface in Afghanistan's new political framework, like a bomb waiting to explode. Ultimately, what the Loya Jirga produced was not a constitution for all time, but a constitution for Karzai.

The selection of the president and the parliament

The holding of a presidential election on 9 October 2004 was a remarkable achievement, and the mounting of Wolesi Jirga and Provincial Council elections on 18 September 2005 even more so. Elections are logistically the most complicated events that can be undertaken in peacetime, engaging the bulk of the adult population, over a short period of time, in an event which must be marked by a high degree of security. Where elections are concerned, a number of specific requirements for "freedom" and "fairness" have been developed. "Freedom," write political scientists Jørgen Elklit and Palle Svensson, "entails the right and the opportunity to choose one thing over another." This implies the absence of coercion of voters. Key freedoms (for both voters and candidates) include freedom of movement, assembly, association, and speech, as well as universal adult franchise and freedom from intimidation. "Fairness," they argue, means impartiality, and "involves both *regularity* (the unbiased application of rules) and *reasonableness* (the not-too-unequal distribution of relevant resources among competitors)." Criteria for fairness include independent electoral authorities, impartial voter education, fair media access, secure polling stations and ballot boxes, and appropriate, transparent, and reviewable scrutiny procedures.[34] The need to meet these criteria is one reason why establishing defensible electoral processes tends to be time-consuming and laborious. As a report to the UN secretary-general presciently observed, "Elections that are not properly prepared and that are held without the best possible conditions first being established often lead to 'token' democracies and radicalized politics, and undermine compromise among stakeholders and coalition-building. This is particularly relevant in situations where rule-of-law institutions are weak and incapable of managing political debate and conflict."[35]

The presidential election was in practice a less challenging management task. Most importantly, the voting system ordained by the constitution allowed the same ballot paper to be used throughout the country. The conduct of the election was in the hands of the Joint Electoral Management Body, which brought together local and international staff: its secretary was Dr Farouq Wardak, who had headed the secretariat for the Constitutional Loya Jirga, and its principal technical adviser was Professor Reginald Austin, who had been chief electoral officer at the 1993 Cambodian elections. Large-scale violence on polling day was avoided, Afghan electoral staff discharged their responsibilities for the most part with great care, and while there were problems with the application of indelible ink used to prevent multiple voting,[36] these were not nearly on a scale that could have affected the final outcome. President Karzai enjoyed all the advantages of incumbency. Winning 55.4 per cent of the vote, he easily avoided the need for a run-off election, outclassing his closest rival, Younos Qanuni, with 16.7 per cent, by almost 40 percentage points. While the official turnout figure was 69.2 per cent, the "real" turnout may have been much higher, since a considerable amount of anecdotal evidence suggested that the estimated number of registered voters had been significantly inflated by multiple registration. Qanuni's candidature further demonstrated the fluidity of Afghan political affiliations. Foreign Minister Abdullah, whom many would have depicted as Qanuni's soul mate, remained studiously neutral in public and Karzai, who had appointed a surviving brother of Ahmad Shah Massoud as one of his vice-presidential running mates (in place of Fahim), encountered no opposition from either the Massoud family or former President Rabbani.

President Karzai understandably greeted the result as supplying him with a significant popular mandate and moved to restructure his cabinet. He also turned his mind to how parliamentary elections should be conducted. While the constitution was specific as to how a president should be chosen, it was silent as to the electoral system for the Wolesi Jirga. In divided societies with fragile state structures, there is much to be said for systems that award seats to different forces in proportion to their electoral support. President Karzai rejected this option in favour of the system known as the "single non-transferable vote," or SNTV. Under this system, seats are allocated to provinces in accordance with their estimated populations, voters simply vote for a single candidate at province level, and seats are allocated to individual candidates in order of the number of votes received. The virtue of the system is its simplicity for voters; its great weakness is its potential to produce perverse outcomes.[37] If, for example, a strong, moderate candidate emerged in a province with ten seats and won 90 per cent of the vote, he or she would still only win one seat. The remaining 90 per cent of seats would be allocated to candidates who *in total* secured only 10 per cent of the votes.

The SNTV system may have appealed to the president not just because of its simplicity, but because it weakens the position of organised political parties. Although political parties come in various forms and can operate in positive as well as negative ways,[38] the hostility of Karzai and his associates towards them seemed deep-rooted. Under SNTV, parties need exceptionally sophisticated and disciplined supporters who can be divided into "blocs" for the purpose of supporting the different candidates a party might put forward in a province. Otherwise, it is more than likely that the bulk of votes cast for a party will go to its leading candidate, and that many of these votes will in effect be "wasted." The result is likely to be a chamber of independents, with at best a few loose blocs. This was what Afghanistan experienced after the parliamentary elections of 1965 and 1969.[39] Few members brought a national vision to politics; many focused simply on extracting what resources they could from the state bureaucracy in the hope that they would be re-elected (or live more comfortably if they were not). There is a real risk that the "need for solidarity amongst Pushtuns" will at some point be promoted to forge a core bloc of parliamentary supporters for the president. This would be a dangerous development, as it would likely trigger an intensification of politicised identification along ethnic lines among non-Pushtuns as well.

The Wolesi Jirga elections of September 2005 vindicated expectations of a messy outcome, although it remains to be seen exactly what the specific political consequences will be. The most positive dimension was the performance of women. The constitution guaranteed that 68 out of 249 members would be women, but nineteen women won seats without the need for constitutional assistance, and in Herat a woman, Fawzia Gailani, topped the poll. It will be interesting to see whether women members come to form a bloc of their own, for a very detailed study of the results by Andrew Wilder suggests that the Wolesi Jirga is highly fragmented on other lines. He calculates that the 249 members comprise 81 who are "pro-government," 84 who are "pro-opposition," and 84 who are non-aligned. Using criteria related to ideological orientation, he classifies the 249 members as consisting of 66 who are "conservative/fundamentalist," 47 who are "moderate/traditionalist," 43 who are "liberal/left," and 93 who are independent. Looking at ethnicity, his study suggests that the Wolesi Jirga contains 118 Pushtuns (47.4 per cent), 53 Tajiks or Aimaqs (21.3 per cent), 30 Hazaras (12.0 per cent), 20 Uzbeks (8.0 per cent), and 28 others. Somewhat more ominously, Wilder quotes one analysis to the effect that the new National Assembly "will include 40 commanders still associated with armed groups, 24 members who belong to criminal gangs, 17 drug traffickers, and 19 members who face serious allegations of war crimes and human rights violations."[40]

One disturbing feature of the election was the turnout. The total turnout for the Wolesi Jirga election was only 49.4 per cent, a very significant fall from the figure less than a year earlier at the presidential poll. In Kabul, the figure was just 33 per cent. The "novelty" of 2004 was missing, of course, and given the strongly presidential character of the system, some voters may have felt that they had already chosen their leader and had no need to go out to vote again. It was also the case that many candidates were completely unknown to the public (and others who were well known were not well liked). But that said, there is anecdotal evidence of disillusionment with Karzai,[41] and the Afghan government would do well to take it very seriously. It is certainly something that will be exploited by the opposition in the new Wolesi Jirga.

When a new constitution is devised, one of the first tests of its effectiveness is how well the different roles it creates fit together. To prevent the emergence of tyrannical rule, there is much to be said for separating legislative, executive, and judicial powers, along the lines defended by writers such as Montesquieu.[42] But it is also important to avoid confusing overlap in responsibilities, for this can generate debilitating conflicts as different institutions struggle for control of particular issues. This is a pressing matter when a constitution creates both a presidency and a parliament. If Karzai proves a less-than-vigorous initiator of policy, then it is likely that some forces within the new legislature will seek to fill the vacuum. However, the National Assembly does not have the power to prevent the adoption of the state budget,[43] and on the whole is a rather weak body – perhaps unfortunately so, given the virtues of strong legislatures.[44]

This therefore throws a heavy burden onto Karzai's personal office.[45] To work effectively, such an office must be coherently organised. Some presidents thrive on an environment in which their immediate advisers have overlapping responsibilities. At best, this can generate a Socratic dialogue which advances the president's understanding of complex issues, as different advisers offer diverse perspectives on the same issue. But this depends upon the president's having a clear sense of priorities. The danger is that the president will be bewildered by complexity, and will respond to the pressures of the last adviser with whom he spoke. In Afghanistan, it would be best if policy advisers to the president had carefully demarcated responsibilities, to minimise the danger of fruitless and confusing politicking. The president's office must also be bureaucratically efficient. With the president at the apex of the system, it is essential that proper records be kept of his meetings, that policy papers be circulated to the appropriate recipients in a timely fashion, that all decisions be minuted, and that line ministries be properly informed about key decisions. And the office must be properly staffed. Officers must be selected on account of their competence, rather than partisan, ethnic, or family ties, and they must have job descriptions that identify their specific tasks and guide them as to what they must do on a day-to-day basis.

Establishing new bureaucracies

The problem of constituting an effective office for the president is simply one aspect of a much broader problem, namely how to constitute appropriate bureaucratic agencies for the new Afghanistan. The concept of bureaucracy is usually traced back to the writings of the German social theorist Max Weber, but its antecedents are much more venerable, and the phenomenon of "bureaucracy" more ancient still.[46] Nonetheless, Weber's analysis provides a good starting point for an understanding of bureaucracy as an ideal type. While he offered various formulations at different times, six features of bureaucracy stood out. First was "the principle of fixed and official jurisdictional areas, which are generally ordered by rules, that is, by laws or administrative regulations." Second, the "principles of office hierarchy and of levels of graded authority mean a firmly ordered system of super- and subordination in which there is a supervision of the lower offices by the higher ones." Third, the "management of the modern office is based upon written documents ('the files') which are preserved in their original or draught [sic] form." Fourth, "Office management, at least all specialized office management – and such management is distinctly modern – usually presupposes thorough and expert training." Fifth, when the office is "fully developed, official activity demands the full working capacity of the official, irrespective of the fact that his obligatory time in the bureau may be firmly delimited." Sixth, the "management of the office follows general rules, which are more or less stable, more or less exhaustive, and which can be learned."[47] These conditions were central to Weber's conception of bureaucratic service as a vocation.

In Afghanistan, bureaucracy in Weber's sense is a decidedly unfamiliar phenomenon. The old state bureaucracy before 1978 was one of the most corrupt in human history, and in no sense represented a model for emulation. Nor did the "party-state" system that prevailed under Soviet tutelage after 1978. So Afghan ministers in the post-Bonn era had precious little on which they could draw as inspiration for how agencies should be structured and staffed. As was noted earlier, the shape of the government was driven by the perceived need to award political actors with positions, rather than by a rational appraisal of what an Afghan government should be doing. The staffing of the ministries that resulted from this dysfunctional process did not have much to commend it either. The Independent Civil Service Commission foreshadowed in the Bonn agreement was intended to provide a "sieving" process so that the basic criterion of ability to perform a task would not be overlooked when staffing decisions were being made. But in practice this body, constituted in June 2003 as the "Independent Administrative Reform and Civil Service Commission," proved to be one of the weakest institutions of the Afghan government. As of 2005, it was staffed at "one third of its projected complement."[48]

As a consequence, while hard data are difficult to obtain, it is clear to even the most casual observer that connections rather than ability have governed the selection of a great many appointees.

There are some very able and dedicated Afghans working in central agencies, but too often their time and energy are wasted by others who lack the ability to contribute to the workings of a modern government. The result is an odd situation in which agencies on paper appear to reflect the key features of Weberian bureaucracy, but in practice combine some features of modern bureaucracy with informal networks of patronage. What complicates this picture even further is that while some influential patrons are ministers promoting personal associates with whom they feel comfortable, other patrons are outside the government and use various forms of leverage to place their clients in important positions. This can make it extremely difficult to remove certain staff even if they prove to be incompetent.

A further perverse feature of the new bureaucratic structure also deserves mention. Public sector pay is extremely low: even a very senior official receives only the equivalent of US$298 a month in base salary and allowances.[49] Because there is no shortage in Kabul of positions paid at vastly higher rates, retaining quality staff is difficult. The World Bank has highlighted the problem resulting from the existence of what it calls a "second civil service" of "NGOs, consultants, advisors and employees of UN and other international agencies, including expatriate consultants and Afghans attracted by relatively high salaries."[50] Some of the most gifted young Afghans have gravitated to this sector, and while some equally talented Afghans have remained in state agencies (either through a sense of personal commitment or because independent wealth allows them to do so), the consequence has been an oversupply in public agencies of those who are not particularly gifted but benefit from patronage. The result of this is a peculiarly vicious cycle. Western donors are in general more comfortable funding agencies with which they are familiar; this leads to a flow of monies directly to elements of the "second civil service"; and this in turn stunts the development of the new state, discouraging donors from committing funds to its charge. In 2004–05, again according to the World Bank, around three-quarters of expenditure "was donor-executed, in the external budget, with very limited Government oversight."[51] This, of course, has political ramifications: the government's ability to boost its standing by being seen to be doing good is limited if other actors in effect claim the credit, and good governance is not enhanced when the "second civil service" is not transparent.[52] In other words, the capacity of the state, both real and perceived, will depend not only on how it is structured, but also on how its activities are financed; and the legitimacy of political actors will in significant part depend on the degree of control they can exercise over "state-like" activities. This issue, intimately connected with the attitudes that "rescuers" bring to their activities, is a deeply troubling one for Afghanistan, and I will return to it in more detail in chapter four.

Expanding the writ of the state

Despite its high level of social complexity, Afghanistan has never had a federal system of government, and the very idea of federalism is not well understood. In a federal system, there are at least two levels of government, one of which is central, and the other based at state or provincial level. By constitutional provision, neither the central nor the peripheral components can be unilaterally eliminated except by constitutional amendment, and the constitution apportions power between them. The judiciary is responsible for adjudicating if disputes arise as to which level enjoys ultimate responsibility in particular spheres. When the new constitution was being drafted, however, many Afghans equated federalism simply with "warlord power," and Pushtuns in particular opposed it. Thus, as noted earlier, the Afghan state is a unitary one. The consequence is that authorities in Kabul bear formal responsibility for happenings in even remote and inaccessible parts of the country, and this has the potential to affect the way in which the central government is viewed. Meeting the expectations of those who live in these outlying areas is one of the most daunting challenges for President Karzai and his associates. The authority of Kabul is gradually expanding, but at different paces in different parts of the country, and in some parts very slowly indeed.

For most ordinary Afghans, it is the condition of the trenches and the dispersed field offices of the state that matter most. Kabul is remote and unfamiliar. But in many parts of Afghanistan the trenches and dispersed field offices either do not exist at all, or exist only as bare skeletons with scant capacity to penetrate society, regulate social relationships, or mobilise resources. Enhancing the capacity of the outlying branches of the state is therefore of great importance if a state-building project is to succeed. This is a matter not just of abstract theoretical interest but of immediate and practical importance. When the trenches and the dispersed field offices of the state are weak, other actors can flourish. Some of these may enjoy local legitimacy, which is the case in parts of northern and western Afghanistan. Others are spoilers, who threaten the lives of ordinary Afghans as a way of symbolising the limitations of the new state. This is the case in significant parts of southern and eastern Afghanistan, especially in the provinces of Zabul, Kandahar, Uruzgan, and Helmand.

The populations of these troubled areas have lived without the state for many years, and do not have high expectations of what the state can do for them. But one thing they do expect is that it will supply them with security, and its ability to do so will powerfully shape its legitimacy. How the new state has gone about the difficult task of restoring security is the subject of the next chapter.

CHAPTER 3

Rebuilding security

I n the days after 4 January 2004 there was much celebration in Kabul that the new constitution had at last been finalised. But elsewhere, Afghans had more immediate concerns. On 6 January, a large bomb exploded in Kandahar, killing sixteen people and wounding dozens, including children. That same night, twelve civilians from the Hazara ethnic group were set upon by miscreants. As the *New York Times* reported, "The civilians were villagers among a group of 20 traveling from their home in Kijeran in Oruzgan Province south through Helmand to the provincial capital Lashkar Gah, witnesses said. They had stopped for the night at a small hotel when at 10 p.m. gunmen surrounded the building and broke in, tying the hands of the travelers. They took the 12 men outside, up a small hill and executed them, the witnesses said."[1] Tragically, this atrocity is only one of a large number. On 25 June 2004, a further such attack took place. Agence France-Presse reported it in the following terms:

> KABUL, June 28 (AFP) – Most of the 16 people killed in a bloody attack by suspected Taliban in south-central Afghanistan were recently returned refugees who wanted to participate in upcoming elections, the government said Monday.
>
> The group was pulled from their vehicle in Uruzgan province on Friday and shot dead, apparently for carrying voter registration cards, according to officials.

"Most of the 16 were Hazara people. They had recently returned from Iran," Interior Ministry spokesman Lutfullah Mashal told AFP, referring to the minority ethnic group.

"Most of them had registration cards and some of them were due to get registration cards and participate in the elections."

The scale of violence by which ordinary Afghans are threatened is not widely appreciated in western circles. In contrast to the carnage in Baghdad, which has filled television screens in the west on an almost daily basis and is extensively documented,[2] violence in Afghanistan has generally occurred outside the capital, in areas where media coverage is sporadic. Yet while Afghanistan may not be the Hobbesian space that Iraq has become, the grief that such violence brings for the victims' loved ones is agonisingly real. For that reason, the need to restore meaningful security is central to ensuring a successful transition from the disorder of the past. Indeed, it is so important that some scholars would argue that promoting security should be the dominant objective of interventions, at the expense of more ambitious "state-building" goals.[3]

Dimensions of "security"

The concept of "security" is not as straightforward as it might initially appear. Security *for whom*, and *from what*? Much discussion of security, in the realist tradition of international relations scholarship, is concerned with the security of the territorial state from external attack.[4] For Afghanistan, this is not a trivial concern given the unsettled character of its neighbourhood, but it is by no means the only kind of security worth discussing. More recently, a discourse of "human security" has developed, refocusing the idea of security.[5] The language of "human security" is potentially very useful, because it can help draw attention to threats of violence that may be experienced daily by groups such as women or ethnic minorities even though the state may appear to be secure from external threat.

The discussion of human security began in the late 1980s,[6] has been used in analyses of the Afghan refugee population,[7] and has taken a number of directions. One school of human security thinking, associated with the UN Development Program's 1994 *Human Development Report*, grounds human security in seven values: economic security, food security, health security, environmental security, personal security, community security, and political security.[8] Another school of thought, associated with the former Canadian foreign minister Lloyd Axworthy, has focused more on threats to human security resulting from violent conflict rather than underdevelopment.[9] But perhaps the most basic element of human insecurity is associated with the breakdown of structures that are designed to protect ordinary people from assaults such as those that struck down innocent Afghans in January 2004. As Thomas Hobbes famously put it, "For as the nature of Foule weather, lyeth not in a showre or two of rain; but in an inclination thereto of many dayes together: So the nature of Warre, consisteth not in actuall fighting; but in the known disposition thereto, during all the time there is no assurance to the contrary."[10] Restoring state capacity to provide such assurance is not only central to improving the lives of the people of Afghanistan; it is also central to the identity claims of "the state" for, as Max Weber put it, the "claim of the modern state to monopolize the use of force is as essential to it as its character of compulsory jurisdiction and of continuous operation."[11]

The sphere of the state on which attention has naturally focused is the so-called "security sector," and "security sector reform" has become a buzzword in "post-conflict transitions." The definition of security sector is to some degree arbitrary, but usefully embraces four elements: forces authorised to use force; security management and oversight bodies; justice and law enforcement institutions; and non-statutory security forces, including "liberation armies; guerrilla armies; private bodyguard units; private security companies; and political party militias."[12] In Afghanistan this would embrace the national army and defence ministry; the national police and the interior ministry; the intelligence services; the border control authorities; and those prosecutorial, judicial and penal agencies responsible for dealing with criminal behaviour. My main focus is on the first two of these. The term "security sector" can also embrace the armed groups associated with the anti-Taliban forces (although not, of course, resurgent anti-state militants) and, importantly, it embraces private security companies, widely employed by western agencies in Kabul, which are not well regulated under international law.[13] Finally, it embraces external security actors such as the Coalition forces deployed as part of Operation Enduring Freedom, the International Security Assistance Force, and Provincial Reconstruction Teams deployed in different parts of the country. These international forces, however, do not fall within the direct agenda of security sector reform, although they are certainly relevant to the question of how security sector reform actually evolves.

Security sector reform is a complex process, and can embrace a range of components: disarmament, demobilisation, and reintegration of former combatants; the establishment and deployment of new military and police forces; the establishment of civilian authority over the security sector; and the implementation of devices to make security sector organs more broadly accountable. But the political contexts of security sector reform programs will differ from country to country,[14] and exactly *how* to implement security sector reform is itself a matter of some debate. On the one hand, there is much to be said for the proposition that a holistic vision should underpin it: without a long-term vision and a focus on integrated change, reform simply will not prove sustainable.[15] On the other hand, it can be argued that the holistic approach is over-optimistic, and that one should strive instead for security sector reform that is "more modest and circumspect, and therefore more achievable in its goals," as security analysts Eric Scheye and Gordon Peake put it.[16] A circumspect approach should respond to local needs rather than seek to impose a one-size-fits-all model. The challenge for policy-makers is to meld the wisdom of the holistic approach with the reality of incremental change in a resource-scarce environment. Reconciling these imperatives in the face of ongoing threats to human security has been one of the most daunting challenges that the Afghan authorities and their backers have had to face. It has not been helped by the fragmentation of effort arising from the use of the "lead nation" model, with the United States carrying prime responsibility for reconstructing the army, Germany responsible for police reform, the United Kingdom responsible for counter-narcotics, Italy responsible for judicial reform, and Japan responsible for disarmament, demobilisation, and reintegration of combatants.

Threats to security

As a prelude to examining the complexities of the security sector and of security sector reform, it is useful to explore in more detail some of the particular security threats that haunt the lives of Afghans. These threats come in diverse forms, and have implications for the tasks security sector organs must address, and the ways in which they should seek to perform those tasks.

The revival of Taliban attacks is the most palpable, and in important ways the most disturbing, threat to security in Afghanistan. In the immediate aftermath of Operation Enduring Freedom, the Taliban were scattered, and obliterated as a regime. They were not totally eliminated, however, with key leaders reportedly escaping from the al-Qaeda stronghold at Tora Bora in December 2001;[17] and following the Coalition's inconclusive Operation Anaconda in eastern Afghanistan in March 2002, it was reported that the Taliban were regrouping.[18] But it took the murder near Kandahar on 27 March 2003 of an expatriate Red Cross delegate, Ricardo Munguia, to focus attention on the scale of the problem, which in southern and eastern Afghanistan was serious and growing.[19] Attacks on aid workers, travellers, ethnic minorities, and school teachers are politically potent not because the victims are politically important, but because the very fact that the attack occurs symbolises the inability of the central state to discharge a core function, namely to protect civilians from attacks of this sort. With the passage of time, it became clear that much of the Taliban leadership had crossed into Pakistan, regrouped with some of their foot soldiers, and were using Pakistani sanctuaries as operating bases and recruitment centres for "second generation" Taliban.[20] Pakistan, of course, houses significant networks of Islamic radicals, and some are quite tightly connected to the Taliban.[21]

President Musharraf's attempts to control radical groups and the colleges (*madrassas*) in which they are trained have been sporadic at best.[22] As a result, the re-emergence of the Taliban has gone largely unchecked by the Pakistani state.[23] Indeed, while some see the "neo-Taliban" as beyond Pakistan's capacity to control, the largely peaceful conduct of Afghanistan's presidential election on 9 October 2004 – a poll the Taliban had every reason to disrupt but Washington was desperate to see proceed smoothly – suggests that Pakistan can turn the Taliban on and off like a tap.[24] This is certainly the view of large numbers of level-headed officials in the Karzai government, and explains why their patience in the face of Pakistan's sustained duplicity over its policies towards Afghanistan has nearly run out.

It is tempting to see rising violence in the south of Afghanistan in 2004 and 2005 as a local reaction among Pushtuns against the strength in Kabul of other ethnic groups, or as evidence that the United States and its allies have outstayed their welcome. However, the level of violence in the south has grown as the influence of non-Pushtuns in Kabul has waned – by late 2005, the president, defence minister, finance minister, and chief justice were all Pushtuns – and the Coalition forces in Afghanistan have for the most part been cautious in their use of force, although on a number of occasions they have displayed severe political and cultural insensitivity.[25] While there is growing frustration on the part of members of key Pushtun tribes about the absence of clean and effective rule,[26] a more plausible interpretation is that the rising violence in the south is largely transnational in character,[27] a product of Pakistan's alarm at the influence in the Afghan government of nationalist Pushtuns, for whom the old "Pushtunistan" dispute that contaminated relations between the two states in the early 1960s might still have some sentimental pull.[28] Some combatants are driven by genuine beliefs, others by the offer of money. Dealing with infiltration from Pakistan is further complicated by the porous nature of the Pakistan–Afghanistan border, by the tensions between the Pakistan military and Baluch nationalists,[29] and by the deeper paranoia that Pakistani leaders entertain about cordial relations between Afghanistan and India.[30] What is clear is that the threat posed by the Pakistan-based Taliban is not one Afghanistan can manage on its own: a remedy, if there is one, will be found in attention to the interlocking security problems of South and West Asia rather than in a simple bolstering of Afghanistan's security sector, although an enhanced capacity to police the border regions would certainly help.[31]

A second form of security threat is posed by local potentates with arms at their disposal. While some so-called "warlords" – for example Ismail Khan in Herat before his removal on 11 September 2004 – on occasion proved quite effective in creating a relatively secure local environment, others battled for supremacy against local rivals in a way that threatened those caught in the crossfire; the complex tensions in the Mazar-e Sharif area between Abdul Rashid Dostam and Atta Muhammad come to mind. Furthermore, in the wake of the removal of the Taliban regime, serious pogroms occurred against ethnic Pushtuns in northern Afghanistan at the hands of local power holders.[32] But the most dangerous "warlords," as I suggested earlier, are not so much the well-known regional strongmen of the past in the north and west, but the larger number of smaller and less well-known leaders of armed groups currently active in the south and east. Their presence in part accounts for the relative weakness of the state in these parts of the country[33] – assuming that they have not already penetrated the state for their own nefarious ends. A classic collective action problem, warlordism must be addressed not simply by deployment of security forces, but by a synoptic process of state consolidation, combined with the promotion of social norms that militate against it, and on occasion the creation of personalised incentives for behaviour modification. The replacement of Ismail Khan, whatever its long-term consequences, is probably not the model to use; it was carried off relatively smoothly in part because Ismail's mind was elsewhere: at the time when Karzai moved against him with Ambassador Khalilzad's support, he was mourning his son, who had been killed shortly before. All this again highlights the danger of making sweeping generalisations about "warlordism."

A third security threat, often overlooked, is arguably more significant than warlordism, although to some degree it overlaps with the kind of warlordism found in the south and east. It is the threat posed by criminality, often the security threat that most regularly blights the day-to-day lives of ordinary people. Here, it is important to distinguish between two different kinds of criminal activity. On the one hand, people can be threatened by petty banditry carried out by sundry crooks, thugs and thieves. This exists, on varying scales, as a problem in virtually all societies, and is best addressed by enhanced policing capacity. On the other hand, threats of a very different kind can come from organised criminal groups, some of which may be transnational in character. While they come in different shapes and sizes – according to the criminologist Louise I. Shelley there is no "prototypical crime cartel"[34] – they can pose an altogether more intractable problem.

Networks of this sort are dangerous for a range of reasons. First, they are much more difficult to hit than the petty criminal, since the leaderships and middlemen are often remote from the theatre of criminal activity. They thrive on poverty, which means that low-level operatives can easily be replaced by others desperate to find ways of supporting their families. Second, their assets are often spread across a number of countries, requiring complex coordination if they are to be sequestered. Third, some groups may have enough resources at their disposal to corrupt the embryonic policing and other bureaucratic structures of an infant state.[35] The most notorious groups of this kind are those networks involved in the production and trafficking of narcotics, a booming industry in Afghanistan. And one fear that has surfaced is that Afghanistan could actually become a "narco-state," defined by the former aid worker Matt Weiner as "a state where drug networks are able to control and regulate the coercive instrumentalities of the state, financial apparatus and government executive and policy to facilitate narcotics production, refining and trafficking."[36] The fear may be exaggerated (or at least premature), but it is not spurious or fanciful. Problems of this sort, again, cannot be addressed simply by enhancement of the security sector. They are complex challenges, requiring subtle and integrated responses.

Transitional security instruments

In its initial phase in October–November 2001, Operation Enduring Freedom relied on air power and small teams of special forces supplied by the United States, in combination with far larger numbers of ground troops who were local Afghan opponents of the Taliban, especially followers of the late Ahmad Shah Massoud.[37] This reflected the difficulty of shifting large numbers of troops into a rugged and landlocked country, as well as caution about the reception such forces would receive in a country that the Soviet Union had found so inhospitable after the December 1979 invasion. But Afghanistan in 2001 was not the same country it had been in 1979, and once the interim administration was established it supported an expanded US ground presence. Thus, over time, the Coalition forces deployed as part of the ongoing Operation Enduring Freedom – not just US soldiers but also small contributions from US allies including the United Kingdom and Australia – increased significantly. The US contingent slowly expanded from around 8000 in 2002 to 11,000 in 2004, and then was boosted to over 20,000 as the presidential election approached,[38] a figure around which it has continued to hover. A 2005 study suggested that the incremental cost of US operations in Afghanistan was between US$900 million and US$1 billion per month.[39]

The core of the Coalition structure is the Combined Forces Command headed by a US lieutenant-general, which was based first at Bagram air base and from late 2003 near the US embassy in Kabul. The Bagram base, and a base at Kandahar airport, are two of the most important Coalition bases, with many smaller units operating elsewhere. The Coalition forces are a key instrument of transitional security, providing the core units to deal with remaining Taliban and al-Qaeda cells, and also acting as something of a tripwire by discouraging Pakistan from fomenting activities that could affect its relations with major western powers.

The second major (approved) foreign presence in Afghanistan is the NATO-led International Security Assistance Force, or ISAF.[40] This force, a product of the Bonn agreement and of UN Security Council Resolution 1386 of 20 December 2001, was given an enforcement mandate under Chapter VII of the Charter of the United Nations. It was initially not under the command of NATO, for the principal focus of NATO (the North Atlantic Treaty Organisation) had long been European security – with the objective, as one cynic put it, of keeping America in, Russia out, and Germany down. But ISAF – initially under British, then Turkish, then German and Dutch command – was brought under NATO command on 11 August 2003, and there it is likely to stay. The initial hope of the United Nations, Karzai, and many Afghans was that ISAF would rapidly be expanded from Kabul to other urban centres in Afghanistan, creating both a sense of momentum in the post-Taliban transition and a degree of ambient security for ordinary Afghans. That this did not happen was one of the worst blunders in post-Taliban Afghanistan, and it was only in October 2003, through Security Council Resolution 1510, that ISAF received a wider mandate. The United States bore prime responsibility for this error: Vice-President Cheney openly rejected ISAF expansion,[41] essentially to conserve airlift assets for future use against Iraq. As one expert US study put it, "After the United States refused to provide airlift, intelligence, and extraction support, the proposal died."[42]

By late 2005, ISAF numbered around 9000 troops – over 2000 each from Germany and Italy, with substantial contributions from Canada, Spain, and France, and smaller contributions from more than 30 other countries, not all of them NATO members – and plans were under way for a significant further expansion of NATO's contribution in southern Afghanistan.[43] ISAF's main achievement has been to stabilise the environment in Kabul. This has been largely a result of the deployment of the ISAF Multinational Brigade, comprising around 2000 French and German troops as well as smaller units from other countries. ISAF patrols the city, and has been warmly welcomed by Kabul residents, not least because heavily armed Afghan groups have been eased out of

Kabul as a result of the ISAF presence. While from time to time there have been significant attacks, such as a car bombing near the Spinzhar Hotel in downtown Kabul which claimed over 30 lives and left over 160 wounded on 5 September 2002, these remain isolated incidents rather than daily perils. Kabul is not an easy city in which to live, but it is no Baghdad.

The blocking of the expansion of ISAF triggered an interesting, if controversial, experiment in security operations: the deployment of what came to be known as Provincial Reconstruction Teams, or PRTs. An outgrowth of much debate in recent years over the appropriate form of civil–military cooperation in disrupted states,[44] the PRT model was seen as an ad hoc device for marrying security and reconstruction in more remote parts of Afghanistan. The deployment of the teams began in Gardez in January 2003, and further Coalition teams were then sent to Bamiyan and Kunduz. By late 2005, there were no fewer than 22 PRTs in different parts of Afghanistan. Thirteen of these were under the auspices of the Coalition Combined Forces Command, in Bamiyan, Parvan, Mehtarlam, Asadabad, Jalalabad, Khost, Gardez, Dharana, Ghazni, Qalat, Tarin Kot, Kandahar, and Lashkar Gah, with the United States, New Zealand, and South Korea taking lead roles in the PRTs' operations. Nine were under ISAF auspices, in Mazar-e Sharif, Maimana, Kunduz, Faizabad, Pul-e Khumri, Herat, Farah, Qala-e Naw, and Chaghcharan, with the United Kingdom, Germany, Italy, Spain, Lithuania, Norway, and the Netherlands taking lead roles. Further ISAF PRTs were envisaged for the difficult provinces of Helmand, Kandahar, Uruzgan, and Zabul.

It would be a mistake to think that these teams follow a single model. In some cases little more unites them than their name and the military backgrounds of their key personnel. Teams under US command have given effect to US doctrine on civil–military cooperation, which derives in part from the "hearts and minds" strategy that Field Marshal Sir Gerald Templer pursued in dealing with the Malayan Emergency, and to which US commanders paid at least lip service in Vietnam. The emphasis of US teams has been on supporting local governance structures and implementing "quick impact" development projects. This has earned them the ire of humanitarian relief organisations, which see this as producing a dangerous blurring between the "partisan" activities of the Coalition and "neutral" humanitarian actions. As a US Institute of Peace report puts it, "When international forces are involved in a spectrum of roles that ranges from capturing insurgents and bombing heroin labs to building schools and clinics, confusing messages are sent to the civilian population about the difference between foreign military and civilian roles."[45]

Other teams have approached their tasks quite differently. The New Zealand team in Bamiyan, for example, is much more focused on stabilising the areas in which it works than on undertaking direct delivery of assistance. The New Zealanders have worked very effectively with the local community and provincial governor, driving home the point that developing organic relations with local networks is crucial to success: without alertness to local complexities, a PRT mission can easily go astray.[46] The New Zealand experience, and the British approach in Mazar-e Sharif and Maimana, offer good examples of how the PRT model can best be used. Unlike the US model, they have largely avoided tensions with non-government organisations, and they do not give rise to the problems that "quick impact" projects can foster when developmental actions are not coordinated with wider strategic-developmental goals.

Disarmament, demobilisation, and reintegration of combatants

It is almost a commonplace claim that disarmament, demobilisation, and reintegration of combatants should be a central part of any meaningful process of "post-conflict transition," and there is much to be said for the view that security will be difficult to achieve in a country bristling with arms. But the obstacles to disarmament, demobilisation, and reintegration are substantial, partly because what might appear collectively rational need not make much sense to every individual. It is one thing to recognise the abstract virtue of a situation in which one cannot be coerced by others; it is another thing to agree to relinquish one's coercive capacity if one cannot be sure that others will do the same. The challenge of disarmament and demobilisation is thus caught up in the broader problem of erosion of trust that I noted in chapter one. Furthermore, Professor Nazif Shahrani has argued, and not without some merit, that "disarming local communities is not only dangerous for the long-term security of such communities vis à vis other belligerent and hegemonic forces, and/or oppressive and autocratic central governments, but also for national defence against foreign threats."[47] For this reason, external guarantees of security are often required to lubricate a disarmament process.

The disarmament, demobilisation, and reintegration of combatants is a much more complex process than is often appreciated, and is best seen as part of a wider set of changes. As one scholar has put it, soldiers and armed formations "may be regarded as agents or actors, but these agents are constituted by social structures and processes. From a critical perspective, we should regard soldiers and weapons as part of the processes and institutions in which they are embedded. If we separate them from the structures, processes, interests, values and institutions that constitute them, we isolate them and ultimately mislead ourselves. If we isolate or reify them, we may canton them, confine them, or remove them from particular locations, but we shall still leave the structures and values that constituted them intact."[48] When we examine things from a wider perspective, immediate problems come into view. Is it fair, or wise, or economical to offer combatants rewards for disarming when there may be no rewards for those who never took arms and never threatened anyone? Are purely moral or symbolic rewards likely to prove effective? Is disarmament by coercive means likely to be any more effective? The balances that need to be struck in addressing these questions are delicate, and there are no magic solutions on offer.[49]

In Afghanistan, the management of disarmament, demobilisation, and reintegration has been in the hands of the Afghan New Beginnings Program, auspiced by the UN Development Program with financial support from the government of Japan. The program's principal focus has been on forces attached to supporters of the post-Bonn administrations in Kabul. Initiated in an announcement from

President Karzai on 6 April 2003, it has operated from a head office in Kabul, with eight regional offices, and by the end of August 2005 had spent US$74,466,113 on the disarmament, demobilisation, and reintegration project.[50] Even its most ardent supporters might hesitate to label it an unqualified success, and many assessments would be much harsher. Its main achievement has been the decommissioning of a substantial number of heavy weapons.[51] Beyond this its achievements have been far patchier.

The program has faced a number of difficulties. First, there is a lack of adequate data on the exact nature of the problem to be addressed: which armed persons qualify as "combatants," and how is their status to be substantiated? If material benefits are to be used to induce people to disarm then this is a central issue.[52] A second difficulty is to identify the long-term effects of disarmament, demobilisation, and reintegration. While the New Beginnings Program claimed by the end of 2005 to have disarmed and demobilised over 60,000 people, an imponderable question is whether they will stay demobilised if the broader security situation deteriorates. A third problem relates to the targeting of senior commanders, when often it is lower commanders who are the most important to disarm.[53] A fourth problem relates to a host of armed bands – some 1800 groups, with approximately 125,000 members[54] – that did not fall within the immediate target audience for the New Beginnings Program but still pose security threats. A new process known as Disbandment of Illegal Armed Groups (DIAG) was put in place in July 2005 to address this problem, but its focus on community development projects gives it little appeal for those groups already thriving on illicit economic activities. Furthermore, despite the efforts of the staff of Afghanistan's National Security Council, Afghan political support for the program remains fitful, and this has not been much helped by placing it under a commission headed by Vice-President Karim Khalili. Before the 2005 parliamentary elections, the United Nations identified a substantial number of candidates who should have been disqualified from the polls by virtue of ongoing associations with illegal armed groups; very few were.

There may be a useful parallel to draw between disarmament, demobilisation, and reintegration in a country such as Afghanistan, and arms control more generally. Even during the era of détente, the negotiation of agreements such as the Strategic Arms Limitation Treaty, SALT I, between the United States and the Soviet Union proved agonisingly difficult because of the benefits that could accrue to a party from duplicity. With the Soviet invasion of Afghanistan, this period of arms control negotiation effectively came to an end, and it was only in the Gorbachev era that new progress was made. But the lesson one should take from this is that disarmament largely follows, rather than drives, an improvement in relations between parties. If this is indeed the case, then it may be naive to expect that comprehensive disarmament, demobilisation, and reintegration can be brought about as an act of public policy. Some progress may be achieved, but beyond a certain point it will be developments in the wider spheres of politics and society that determine which disarmament goals can be realised.

Crafting a new army

A long-term strategy of the Afghan government has been the establishment of a new Afghan National Army, or ANA. This is a very important enterprise, for ultimately security forces of this kind are essential if the state is to move towards establishing a monopoly over the legitimate means of violence. The construction of a new army is a complex exercise, however, since it involves not just recruiting and training troops in basic combat techniques, but also identifying the specific roles of the military and developing an organisational culture that will make a force robust rather than fragile.[55] In Afghanistan, forces are needed to help secure the country's borders from foreign infiltrators, help deter threats from the territory of neighbouring states, deal with high-level internal security threats, dispose of the detritus of past armed conflicts, and provide logistical capability to deal with a range of natural threats such as earthquakes, avalanches, and flash floods – the kind of work that is known as "aid to the civil authority." Developing a new army is not simply a matter of training troops; it also raises issues about the broader defence ministry structure in which such an army would be nested. Here, the process of security sector reform was slowed by the reluctance of anti-Taliban forces to relinquish control of a ministry they had initially dominated. Finally, a compromise of sorts was reached in which General Abdul Rahim Wardak, an ethnic Pushtun who had been close to a pro-royalist Mujahideen party during the 1980s, replaced Fahim as defence minister, but a close associate of the late Ahmad Shah Massoud, namely General Bismillah Khan, became army chief of staff.

The United States has been the lead country in the construction of the Afghan National Army. As in Iraq, it has depicted the development of the army as part of a long-term strategy of disengagement, through the development of an indigenous force capable of performing the tasks currently being undertaken by ISAF and the Coalition. In keeping with the importance of building up the ANA, the United States has invested heavily in its creation. In the Afghan budget, the expenditure on the ANA for 2003–04 was estimated at US$797 million, for 2004–05 at US$788 million, and for 2005–06 at US$830 million,[56] most of it coming from various US appropriations. It is highly debatable whether costs on this scale could be sustained by any Afghan government in the foreseeable future, and this brings political risk, for as Barnett R. Rubin has argued, "If the state cannot sustain the recurrent costs of its security forces, its stability will be at risk. Nor can any state long survive the funding of its army and police by foreign powers."[57] That said, there may be a case for external injections of funds to meet one-off, start-up costs for a new military, for otherwise it would be very difficult for such a force even to get off the ground. One temptation that can easily emerge in such a situation is to push for rapid expansion of force numbers, so as to meet the undoubted need for security as swiftly as possible. But there are real risks associated with such an approach. The problem of fast-track training was addressed during the Vietnam war by Sir Robert Thompson, a noted British counterterrorism expert, who warned that if, "because demands are urgent and impatience wins the day, training is reduced and short crash programs are instituted, there will be a constant supply of inexperienced, incompetent, useless officials who will be incapable of implementing any policy and who will merely add to the prevailing confusion."[58]

Despite these significant qualifications, the achievements in building the new Afghan National Army appear to have been considerable. On 2 December 2002, Karzai announced a target of 70,000 for the ANA,[59] although not all of these would be ground troops. Initially, the ANA was plagued by alarmingly high desertion rates, reaching 10 per cent per month in summer 2003, but by mid 2005 this had been reduced to 1.2 per cent per month.[60] That desertion rates were initially high is not surprising; many of the early "recruits" were in effect nominees of armed militias, who would have found the demands of western trainers very different from militia life. Furthermore, many are non-literate: the corps commander in Kandahar, for example, reported in early 2006 that 80 per cent of his soldiers were non-literate, as were 50 per cent of his officers.[61] What may have cut the desertion rate was the improvement in pay: as the World Bank has documented, ANA pay scales easily outstrip those of ordinary bureaucrats and teachers, starting at US$71 a month.[62] Recruits receive fourteen weeks of training, divided into "basic," "advanced individual," and "collective" phases.

The security sector specialist Mark Sedra has given an upbeat assessment of the ANA's achievements: "Despite the many problems that the ANA has faced, it is widely viewed as a 'success story' in the SSR [security sector reform] process, particularly when compared with the state of reform in the police and the judiciary. The ANA has displayed a high degree of discipline, professionalism and combat effectiveness and, due to the institution of ethnic quotas, is largely representative of the country's ethnic composition."[63] The one qualification that should be made to this evaluation is that the ANA is yet to be deployed in a large-scale operation that would seriously test the loyalty of a significant bloc of troops to the army chain of command rather than to people of a specific locality, ethnicity, or *qawm*. Where security forces confront an external enemy, nationalist sentiments may generate cohesion. When the threat is internal, the loyalties of soldiers may be divided, something the Coalition Provisional Authority in Iraq discovered the hard way during the April 2004 Fallujah campaign, when a battalion of the new armed forces declined to play a part in action directed against fellow Iraqis.[64] While elements of the ANA have been deployed in tense situations in Herat and Maimana, their commanders appear – very wisely – to have been reluctant to order them to fire against other Afghans, using them instead as symbolic circuit-breakers.

Developing civilian policing

If the assessment of the work of the Afghan National Army is broadly positive, the same, alas, cannot be said of the Afghan National Police. To understand why this has been the case involves exploring the very distinctive and important roles that civilian police have to play, roles which often receive inadequate attention when the broad paths of political transitions are being planned. A properly functioning civilian police fills the crucial security gap between protection against external and high-level internal threats (for which the army is responsible), and protection against behaviour that is unpleasant but not unlawful (addressed by social norms and people's desire to avoid being shunned if they violate such norms). Police are required to deal with the threat of interpersonal criminality, and the police function has been recognised as a distinctive state responsibility for almost three centuries. In some countries, police forces are paramilitary organisations, and in others they are licensed to use lethal force. However, in many situations, police are unarmed, and community-based. A police system, as one observer has put it, is "an organization made up of groups and individuals, existing for a specific purpose, employing systems of structured activity with an identified boundary."[65] This purpose is to maintain civil order. The civilian police role in a fragmented state includes providing a stable and secure environment; assisting in dismantling the old instruments of repression; establishing and maintaining a law enforcement and criminal investigation capability; undertaking investigations and collecting evidence for the prosecution of alleged serious violations of human rights; assisting in re-establishing the criminal justice system and civil administration, including the court system and the gaols; and confidence-building with the civil community by operating impartially to enforce the law.[66]

Police forces differ from the military in a number of key respects. One of the most important is the use of discretion. Police aim to deliver justice, rather than win a "victory." They are constantly rather than periodically active. They are mainly accountable to judicial rather than executive authority, and their aim is to gather evidence to put before a court. They use minimum rather than graduated force. The focus of police activity is an individual policeman rather than a complex combat unit. They tend to be linked to particular localities, and function best when they have organic links to society.

In Afghanistan, the police have historically been highly politicised, as has the interior ministry, to which the policing function is formally attached. Indeed, from late 2005, following the resignation of the interior minister, Ali Ahmad Jalali, the ministry went for months without a substantive minister in place. The legal framework governing policing was historically weak,[67] and police in Afghanistan also had a history of being highly corrupt: the policing function is typically the activity of the state that it is most rewarding for criminal networks to subvert, and many have the resources to do so. Furthermore, police have not in the past been particularly well paid, heightening the temptation for them to use their powers to extract resources from the wider community as a way of supporting their immediate dependents. Finally, police in Afghanistan, as elsewhere, have been employed as agents of state repression, with various communist police agencies developing fearsome reputations for this very reason.[68]

Bringing about significant reform in the sphere of policing is perhaps the most awkward single task that the government confronts. The individuals who will make up the police force are not cantoned in neat blocks where they can be trained and then monitored; community police by definition are thinly spread throughout the territory of a state, putting most of them, for most of the time, beyond the reach of direct scrutiny. Their isolation means they are exposed to all sorts of pressures that may be exerted by local notables whose coercive power exceeds the institutional power that an individual policeman can immediately mobilise. This is a phenomenon with which observers of policing are all too familiar, and it was brilliantly depicted in the character of Sheriff Horn in John Sturges's 1954 film *Bad Day at Black Rock*.

As noted earlier, Germany has been the lead nation where police reform in Afghanistan is concerned, but the United States has provided significant resources to support the process, to the reported tune of US$860 million for 2005–06.[69] The objective has been to develop a national police of 50,000 (actually consisting of 47,400 "national" police and 2600 "highway" police) and a border police of 12,000, and the principal instrument has been the newly reconstructed Kabul Police Academy. However, the rebuilding of the police has been compromised at numerous levels. On the one hand, new recruits have often had backgrounds that in other countries would have disqualified them from policing roles: as one observer has put it, the "faction leaders and commanders who seized power in late 2001 also took control of police stations and in most cases installed commanders loyal to them as police chiefs. Trained policemen, who had served under previous administrations, were called back to their jobs by the ATA [Afghan Transitional Administration], but few of them hold senior posts and most serve under former *mujaheddin* commanders who lack qualifications for the positions of police chief."[70] On the other hand, pay scales have been very low, and while a new base figure of US$70 a month has been put in place,[71] the delivery of pay is a logistical nightmare, leading one provincial governor to observe that "even an angel cannot be honest" under such conditions.[72] Operations are also compromised by a serious shortage of serviceable vehicles and the difficulty of obtaining fuel for the vehicles they do have.[73] But looming over all these problems has been the substantial absence of on-the-job mentoring as part of police training. It is such experience-based learning, rather than formal training programs, that brings about the proper and effective use of discretion by police in well-functioning police forces.

The "ethos" of the security sector

Although the structural and functional challenges of reforming the security sector are daunting on their own, a deeper set of issues pervades every part of the sector. They pertain to the culture of the security sector in a new Afghanistan. After the turmoil of the last three or so decades, it is understandable that Afghans wish to see a robust state develop which can guarantee them a modicum of personal security; this, after all, is what a "human security" focus is supposed in part to portend. But at the same time, it is important to recall that accountability of the security sector itself is just as important.[74] As the Roman writer Juvenal famously put it, who will guard the guardians themselves (*quis custodiet ipsos custodes*)? Without mechanisms of accountability, and without an appropriate organisational culture, the security sector rapidly becomes part of the problem rather than part of the solution.

An appropriate organisational culture has a number of elements. One is a culture of obedience to law, and to civilian authority as long as it acts as the law requires. This is often a challenge in transitional periods, where the specific content of law may be uncertain or not widely known. Nonetheless, it is important in sustaining the integrity of security forces in fragmented societies. Barnett R. Rubin has argued that the "intense quasi-religious *esprit de corps* of military organisations derives from the human need to believe intensely in something for which one risks one's life. Forming effective armies and police requires formation of a national authority that can command such loyalty, not just technical training. The formation of an officer corps particularly depends on coherence and spirit in service to a mission. Hence, though effective security is necessary to carry out credible elections and other political processes, political processes that build credible, legitimate national leadership are essential to building effective security forces."[75] There is much good sense in this, but one qualification is in order: effective units within a military can also depend on a different logic, one of face-to-face solidarity among individuals who depend upon their immediate fellows if their group is under attack.[76] This, however, is a product of direct involvement in combat, and does not much assist when one's aim is to build solidarity within the security forces in the hope that their manifest strength will deter others from attacking them in the first place.

Cultures do not develop overnight, and it is therefore important if possible to avoid placing new security organs in situations in which the limits of their capacities might be painfully exposed. But if there is not much that the wider world can do directly to promote a new culture of civic accountability in the Afghan National Army and Afghan National Police, there are some negative examples that might be avoided. First, the proliferation of private security services in theatres such as Afghanistan is unhelpful if one wishes to convey the message that the legitimate use of force is a function of the state. In Afghanistan these services have come in forms as varied as the US private security company DynCorp, whose offices were bombed in the Shahr-e Naw district of Kabul on 29 August 2004,[77] and a group of US freelance vigilantes gaoled on 15 September 2004 for running a private prison in which Afghan victims were allegedly tortured.[78] While firms like DynCorp are now established elements of the security landscape, making use of such companies may have unintended or undesirable consequences.[79] Second, it is extremely important that, by precept and example, the wider world conveys the right picture of how organs of the security sector should behave. When prisoners in US custody die in suspicious circumstances and their killers receive only mild punishments, the effect is to signal that the beating of detainees is broadly acceptable, and when US forces burn the bodies of war dead[80] the underlying message is that the constraints of the Geneva Conventions of 1949 do not really matter. Afghan security forces cannot be expected to meet standards from which western militaries depart when it suits them.

CHAPTER 4

Promoting human development

he legacies of disrupted development hang over Afghanistan like a dark cloud. This was an extremely poor country even before the events of the late 1970s drove it into an abyss of social and political disorder. While strong norms of reciprocity provided some protection against destitution, on a whole range of basic indicators life was extraordinarily difficult, marked by low levels of literacy, high infant mortality, shocking maternal health statistics, and misery caused by a range of easily preventable diseases. When the burden of the intervening years – war-related deaths, massive population displacement, and infrastructural damage – is added to this unpromising base, it becomes clear that Afghanistan's rulers face a human development problem of vast proportions.

Mapping the precise dimensions of this problem is not straightforward. There is an acute shortage of reliable social and economic data. The country has never had a comprehensive census, and statistics compiled by the Central Statistics Office lost all value from the late 1970s, not only because most of Afghanistan lay beyond the control of the state, but also because official statistics in Soviet-type systems were routinely manipulated to make the system's performance appear better than it actually was. In the absence of bureaucratic compilation of data, sample surveys are the best devices for social research, but they too rely on sufficient security for a properly constructed sample to be drawn.

Fortunately, international agencies and new institutes such as the Afghanistan Research and Evaluation Unit have gathered evidence with which we can attempt to paint a more detailed picture of current conditions. The most comprehensive collection of data thus far assembled was used to compile the *Afghanistan National Human Development Report 2004*, and its messages were starkly disturbing. Afghanistan's "Human Development Index" was 0.346, placing it 173rd among ranked states, and ahead only of Burundi, Mali, Niger, Burkina Faso, and Sierra Leone. Life expectancy was only 44.5 years, and the adult literacy rate 28.7 per cent (43.2 per cent for men and only 14.1 per cent for women). Annual gross domestic product per capita, on a purchasing-power parity basis, was US$822. The infant mortality rate was 115 per thousand live births, and the "under five" mortality rate was 172 per thousand live births.[1] The World Bank reported a total GDP for 2003 of US$6.9 billion, made up of an "official GDP" of US$4.6 billion, and an "opium GDP" of US$2.3 billion.[2] Behind these bare statistics lie stories of individual misfortune for large numbers of Afghans, for whom daily life is a battle for survival, punctuated not only by personal insecurity but by the deaths of their children in what should be some of the most joyous years of their lives.

It is important to note that poverty has a distinctly gendered dimension, although it is equally important not to lapse into stereotypes when discussing the very complex issue of gender in Afghanistan. An extremely acute observer, Sippi Azarbaijani-Moghaddam, has criticised the ultra-leftist Revolutionary Association of the Women of Afghanistan for doing just that: "Wholeheartedly milking rumors about women under the Taliban, and cashing in on the naiveté of journalists and researchers content to be hoodwinked and manipulated, the association fuels Orientalist notions of veiled Afghan women living in seraglios, jealously guarded by bearded Muslims wielding scimitars."[3] Although this criticism may seem harsh, it is not unfair. But at the same time it is also important to recognise the diverse processes by which poverty has been feminised – through the emergence of households headed by war widows, through female begging and prostitution, or through inadequate access for females to food and other goods over which male heads of household can exercise control. Past attempts to address gender inequality through radical, state-driven reform have had disastrous effects on ordinary women,[4] and there is no case for going down that path again. But without attention to the peculiar and very serious problems that Afghan women confront, human development policies will embody subtle biases that will work against their succeeding. That said, of course, there are many problems of the utmost urgency that confront men and women equally.

The issue of human development is intimately connected with the character of the Afghan economy. Despite the attention "state-building" and "international assistance" have received in recent years, the bulk of the population has survived through years of turmoil by relying on a circular flow of income in a market economy.[5] Yet while this economy continues to function, it is in notable respects dysfunctional, not least because so much of its value is connected to activities the wider world has come to deem illicit. Afghanistan is thus under considerable pressure to move as quickly as possible to what Richard Rose has called a "civil economy" – a market economy with a clear legal framework.[6] What is perhaps most important here is the development of an adequate and enforceable regime of property rights. If a market system is one of exchangeable private property rights, then stability of title to both personal goods and realty is extremely important. It is not, however, a simple issue to address. The enormous population displacement of recent decades has seen land abandoned, occupied by others, and then reclaimed by persons asserting some superior title in the face of occupants in "adverse possession." A thorough study of the problem in 2003 identified significant variations in the pattern of land ownership between different parts of the country, as well as elements of customary law, civil law, religious law, state law, and constitutional law relevant to tenure. Land itself could be government, public, private, communal, or religious.[7] Furthermore, economic activity, especially in the agricultural sector, does not depend on just one factor of production, but rather on diverse inputs – land, water, seeds, fertilisers, labour, animals, and equipment – being available for use at appropriate moments. When one adds to these complexities the different approaches of successive governments to "land reform," culminating in the catastrophic attempt by the communist regime to redistribute land in 1978–79, one gets a sense of just how difficult the process of stabilising title to land might be. These are not simply rural problems. Of an estimated overall population of 23.85 million in 2003, some 28.8 per cent were classified as urban dwellers,[8] and the population of Kabul has swollen enormously since then, from around two million in 2001 to 3.5 million in 2005.[9] Insecurity of land tenure disrupts household life, and also opens the door to oppressive petty corruption by municipal officials.[10] These are problems that require urgent attention.

Basics of human development: health and education

On 13 May 1998 a memorandum of understanding was signed in Kabul between the Taliban "planning minister," Qari Din Muhammad, and the UN Deputy Emergency Relief Coordinator. While it provided some leeway for UN agencies to secure access to vulnerable groups, it proved a public relations disaster for the United Nations, since Article 13, in a section entitled "Access to Health and Education" stated that "women's access to health and education will need to be gradual."[11] This provoked a furious reaction from advocacy groups worldwide, but it also highlighted the importance of health and education not just as key elements of human development, but as sectors in which symbolic struggles for present and future authority could be mounted. They retain that significance to this day: it is no wonder that schools and school teachers have become favoured targets for Taliban attack in Afghanistan's restive south.

Studies of health and education paint an alarming picture. An early post-Taliban report described the health system as being in a state of "near-total disrepair,"[12] with inadequate infrastructure, doctors lacking in key skills, and poorly coordinated, project-based service delivery. According to the *Afghanistan National Human Development Report 2004*, only eleven of the 34 provinces have obstetric care, and maternal mortality is very high, with 1600 deaths per 100,000 live births. Fifty per cent of children under five suffer from chronic malnutrition, and 10 per cent suffer from acute malnutrition. Tuberculosis is widespread, with 72,000 new cases each year, and malaria is extremely common, including the potentially fatal *plasmodium falciparum* strain. Less than one fifth of the rural population enjoys access to safe water.[13] To these one might add the effects of war-related disability, post-traumatic stress disorder, and mental illnesses, which are not well understood in many parts of the country, and for which data identifying the exact scale of the problem are scarce.

The situation in the educational sphere is scarcely better. The gross primary school enrolment ratio was 54.4 per cent in 2003.[14] Yet while to some this might suggest a glass more than half full rather than almost half empty, it is important to note the *Human Development Report*'s observation that "a third of [all] the children are not in school, while the other two-thirds study under mainly primitive conditions."[15] Significant variation exists between provinces, and girls in particular lack effective access to schooling in the southern and eastern provinces where the Taliban are active, although safe access to schools is certainly a problem for boys as well. A World Bank study has concluded that the "quality of education needs to be substantially improved," adding that "the available input indicators (teachers' background, curricula, textbook quality and availability, conditions of physical learning space, time on task, etc.) strongly suggest that quality is generally poor."[16] The country's main centre of higher learning, Kabul University, lost much of its faculty during the 1980s, and became a mine-strewn battleground between 1992 and 1995, a period that also saw much of its library destroyed.

That problems of this scale persist is in no sense an indictment of President Karzai and his colleagues. They almost entirely reflect the burden of long-term underdevelopment, together with the disruption resulting from decades of conflict. In 1972, towards the end of Zahir Shah's four decades on the throne and on the eve of Afghanistan's slide into disorder, there were only 3972 schools in the country, 760,469 pupils, and 21,920 teachers. In the entire country there were only 827 doctors.[17] Furthermore, it is naive to demand that new health and education sectors suddenly spring up. Both these sectors, if they are to function smoothly, depend on the effective integration of a range of components. In the health sector, it is necessary to bring together primary health care networks, appropriate clinical facilities, better training of medical and nursing practitioners, and supply of medical equipment and medications, together with wider education of the public about the benefits modern medicine, including preventive medicine, can offer. In the education sector, it is necessary to combine an understanding of the importance of education with accessible school buildings, trained teachers, and relevant and up-to-date textbooks and course materials, all in the context of conservative social attitudes which may militate against the cost-savings that co-education can generate. None of this is impossible; work by non-government organisations in rural Afghanistan during the 1980s and 1990s provided access for at least some of the population to schools, clinics, and child vaccination. Indeed, a 1997 study showed that the indefatigable Swedish Committee for Afghanistan had been able – even under the most difficult of circumstances – to sustain a network of rural schools for girls in the southern provinces.[18] But progress in these spheres involves difficult issues of coordination, across agencies and between donors and implementers. In the health sector, as a recent RAND study points out, there is no room for quick fixes.[19] The launch of the Back to School campaign in 2002, for example, was as much a political as an educational exercise; while it had the broadly positive effect of emphasising the centrality of education to a meaningful reconstruction process, it led to much work on physical infrastructure, at the expense of attention to teacher training and sustainable arrangements for paying teachers' salaries.

It is also the case that some evidence from other countries points to complex synergies between female empowerment, education in the form of basic literacy, and improved health conditions, especially for newborn children. Here, the case of neighbouring India is striking,[20] and the much-cited situation in the state of

Kerala particularly so. However, the Kerala case is arguably the product of an historically specific set of institutional and cultural arrangements,[21] and for that reason its ready exportability is doubtful. Nonetheless, the role of female agency in Afghanistan should not be overlooked. In some households, women are significantly involved in important decisions about the education of children,[22] and for a long period have been major actors in the delivery of health and education services. Indeed, Afghanistan's health minister in the 1960s was a woman. Enhanced education for women has beneficial health consequences not only for women but also for the children they rear, and boosts their productivity as economic actors; furthermore, improved female health benefits not only women but other members of their households.[23] The Taliban era represented a very serious setback, but a strong case can be made that without the re-involvement of women, health and educational services will remain seriously stunted. Fortunately, in one positive development, women make up a significant proportion of the student body at Kabul University, and Dr Ashraf Ghani, who became chancellor of the university after serving as finance minister, has been actively pressing the cause of gender equity. But that said, Afghanistan still has far to go before gender equity will be achieved, and this is especially the case in rural areas.

Reforming the state's financial capacity

The seriousness of these problems immediately raises the question of what instruments the government has at its disposal to try to address them constructively. The simple answer is that the design of state agencies to perform key economic tasks is itself a work in progress, and that it remains to be seen how effective they will be. Nonetheless, there have been some significant achievements, and they owe a great deal to the energy of Dr Ghani, who had been a notable commentator on the history of the Afghan state[24] and understood the importance of institutional development, as well as the capacities of key international financial institutions such as the World Bank. His very forthright personal style won him enemies, but no one else could have worked as effectively as he did during his period as finance minister from June 2002 to December 2004 to lay the foundations for a rationally functioning, defensible system of public finances.

His inheritance was a dire one. The principal instrument of fiscal management is the Ministry of Finance, which under the June 2005 Public Finance and Expenditure Management Law is the lead agency in the budget development process. Turning the ministry into a more modern agency was an immediate and daunting task. Michael Carnahan, an Australian economist who served as a consultant to Ghani, has painted a vivid picture of the condition of the ministry after the Taliban period: "At the start of 2002 there were no computers in the ministry – the deputy minister in charge of the budget department provided hand-held calculators to line ministry staff to use when preparing their handwritten budget submissions. The treasury system operated a manual ledger system, so no meaningful reconciliation was ever undertaken." He went on: "Anecdotal evidence suggests that the vast majority of the budget was actually not programmed in any conventional sense; rather, it was kept in discretionary funds that were allocated by the finance ministry or the president's office. This provided considerable scope for corruption and, in July 2002, operations of the finance ministry were reportedly under the control of three significant criminal gangs. Senior positions with access to major revenue sources were said to be bought and sold."[25] While the burden of such problems cannot be lifted instantly, Ghani moved to address them by appointing three new deputy ministers with administrative expertise, and by obtaining international technical assistance. To this there was really no alternative, but as Carnahan has noted the disparities in pay between local and international staff proved a source of tension, as it did in other ministries where such discrepancies could be observed.[26]

It remains to be seen whether the improvements wrought by Dr Ghani will prove sustainable. Nonetheless, as an approach to institutional reform in the short term, they paid off, and the returns were reflected in the growing number of positive comments Afghanistan's public finance management attracted, compliments that would have been unthinkable under any previous government. When Karzai replaced Ghani in the December 2004 reshuffle, his government lost its most dynamic reformer.

It is a commonplace that governments can affect economic activity in part through fiscal and monetary policy, with fiscal policy referring to the use of state revenue and expenditure measures to produce desired macroeconomic consequences, while monetary policy reflects state control of the volume of money. To ensure that fiscal policy is both responsible and effective, revenues must be collected and totalled in a systematic way, and expenditures monitored and controlled. As a matter of public trust, it is also vital that there be audit mechanisms in place, to ensure that the state is not simply being looted by those who are in a position to do so. It is particularly important to be able to distinguish different types of expenditure, by sector and according to whether it is capital or current in character. The World Bank in cooperation with other agencies has identified six critical dimensions of a properly functioning public finance management scheme. These are (1) policy-based budgeting; (2) predictability and control in budget execution; (3) accounting, recording and reporting; (4) external scrutiny and audit; (5) comprehensiveness and transparency; and (6) credibility of the budget.[27] The bank's assessment is encouraging: Afghanistan's ratings against the public finance management performance indicators "generally portray a public sector where financial resources are, by and large, being used for their intended purposes as authorized by a budget which is processed with transparency and has contributed to aggregate fiscal discipline."[28]

Mobilising domestic revenue is one of the most difficult tasks the government has faced. Domestic revenues totalled US$129 million in 2002–03, US$208 million in 2003–04 and US$269 million in 2004–05.[29] Many Afghans have lost the habit of paying taxes, and there are also competitors for access to revenue streams. For example, an early point of friction between Ismail Khan in Herat and Dr Ghani in Kabul related to Ismail's garnering of customs revenues from the main border post between Afghanistan and Iran, which was under his control. Nonetheless, this balance has shifted in Kabul's favour: in 2004–05, the central ministries' share of domestic revenue increased to 79 per cent, up from 71 per cent in the previous year. Over the same period, the proportion of domestic revenue derived from taxes increased from 62 per cent to 75 per cent. Taxes on international trade and transactions (mainly import duties) contributed 57 per cent of domestic revenue in 2004–05; the balance of tax revenue came from taxes on goods and services, and on income, profits, and capital gains.[30] But these revenues cover only a fraction of "state-like" expenditure: Afghanistan's total budget consists of a "core budget," comprising ordinary expenditures and a small number of development expenditures funded through special funds to which donors can make contributions (such as the Afghanistan Reconstruction Trust Fund[31]), and a much larger "external budget," nearly three-quarters of the total, which is directly executed by donors.[32] As long as this remains the case, the Afghan state will be subject to significant constraints as an economic actor.

The legal economy: capital mobilisation and entrepreneurship

While the state can be a significant economic force, it is rarely the only one. Even in command economies, market factors of demand and supply have ways of making their presence felt,[33] and legal economies in most countries are based on market relations. The development of the legal economy in Afghanistan is a matter of very considerable importance. For too long, it has suffered from the effects of what Conrad Schetter has called an "economy of violence," where selling one's services to actors who wish to use violence is one way of sustaining one's livelihood: violence itself "becomes a marketable good."[34] Moving towards an economy based on the supply of less threatening goods and services is therefore very important. But what kinds of economies are feasible? The debilitation of the state means that for the foreseeable future it will lack the bureaucratic capacity to engage in substantial mobilisation of resources, and in any case there are strong grounds for being wary of ambitious attempts by states to do so. Social scientists from across the political spectrum have demonstrated the difficulty governments face in making use of the diversified practical knowledge of consumers and producers,[35] and the contribution that markets make to innovation, by rewarding those who take risks in the expectation of returns, is considerable.[36] Where the state can contribute is by developing an appropriate framework of rules and rights to give shape to market relations and transactions, and mechanisms by which rules and rights can be enforced. There are already social norms which ordain that contracts should be honoured, and these have sustained market activity even in the substantial absence of the state; Jonathan Goodhand has used the term "shadow economy" to label this sphere of activity.[37] However, as more complex forms of economic activity are undertaken, these social norms are likely to be increasingly strained, throwing a responsibility onto the state to foster more appropriate frameworks. The absence of a more formal framework can militate against both investment for the long term and local reinvestment of profits from activities that offer a short-term reward.

Markets have been tremendously important in sustaining those Afghans who survived through the 1980s and 1990s. Yet for all that markets are powerful motors of development, it is important to recognise the distorting influences to which markets in Afghanistan are currently exposed.[38] One is the tendency of markets to be oligopolistic rather than strongly competitive, especially when one is talking of larger volumes or values rather than petty trade. A second is the use of political influence as a means of protection, with businessmen aligning with powerful actors. Unlike their counterparts in Indonesia and Malaysia, for example,[39] businesses in Afghanistan must contend not only with the state and bureaucracy but also with power-holders in the de facto administrations which exist in various parts of the country. A third distorting influence is the ubiquity of corruption as a lubricant that business actors can use to pursue their own goals, or to ensure they are relieved of the burden of government scrutiny. One example of the murky, even sordid, connections between government and business was the eviction of poor residents of the Sherpur district of Kabul in September 2003 to make way for the construction of residences of appalling ostentation for members of the political and business elites, buildings which now stand as symbols of the inequalities of power and resources in post-Taliban Afghanistan.[40] None of these examples of market failure is particularly surprising, but they do highlight the importance of work to perfect the framework within which markets operate.

The area of greatest deficiency is the absence of an effective capital market, which is important in fostering investment.[41] The new Afghan Investment Support Agency headed by Dr Omar Zakhilwal, a Canadian-trained economist, represents a positive step, but much remains to be done. In developed economies, there are mechanisms by which the entrepreneurially minded can raise money to finance projects, ranging from bank loans at a commercial rate of interest to share issues through a stock market. Afghanistan not only lacks such institutions, it operates an essentially cash economy. This not only deters investors, but makes tracking transactions for taxation purposes extremely difficult. While laws on central and commercial banking were adopted in September 2003, their impact is yet to be significantly felt. And although a vibrant foreign currency exchange market operates in Kabul, it serves as a cameo of the good and the bad in Afghanistan's transition, with traders wandering a street of north Kabul clutching wads of Afghan currency (and mobile phones with which they assess the state of the market), offering rates of exchange that allow them a profit on the transaction. While foreigners can seek to move money through the Western Union office in Shahr-e Naw, ordinary Afghans are forced to rely on the *hawala* system, where – in its simplest form – a payment to a *hawala* dealer in Kabul (in Afghan currency) triggers a payment of equivalent amount (in some other currency) by a trusted associate of the dealer in some other country on behalf of the client. This allows foreign purchases to be made, and foreign debts to be settled.[42]

Access to credit would have a significant transforming effect on economic activity. In rural areas it could undermine the position of drug traffickers, who have become important sources of credit for at least some of those who grow opium. But its beneficial effects are potentially broader. Certain types of economic activity depend not on huge investments of funds but on the ability of ordinary people to act rationally in their own interest. The National Solidarity Program involves some recognition of this fact, but is directed at funding projects endorsed by local collective institutions rather than by individuals. The ability of Afghans to act innovatively has long been recognised,[43] but many are unable to grasp opportunities through lack of access to funds. This has led to interesting discussion of microcredit options. In a number of countries, microcredit has been successfully made available to enterprising people, very often women. In 2003, the World Bank was involved in establishing a Microfinance Investment and Support Facility for Afghanistan under the rural reconstruction and development ministry to support the operations of microfinance institutions, and various of these institutions are now active in the field, with a surprisingly large number of women clients.[44] But this still leaves a serious gap, relating to finance for medium-sized enterprises which, according to the World Bank, "would be expected to be a major source of employment and a base of industrial development and private sector development in Afghanistan."[45]

A further requirement for the effective revival of a modern legal economy is facilitation of foreign investment. This is not simply a matter of formal law governing such matters as foreign acquisition of equity or access to foreign loans. More importantly, it depends on stability in two spheres: that of the currency, and that of the polity. In the former sphere, Afghanistan has done extremely well. Money in a modern economy is a store of value as well as a medium of exchange, and if governments seek to cover expenditure simply by printing money on a large scale then the consequent inflation will erode its value.[46] Following the January 2003 currency reform, when new afghani notes replaced the old, thoroughly debauched, currency, the Central Bank has maintained a high level of monetary discipline. Figures presented by the World Bank, limited though they are by the points I made earlier about official statistics, suggest that the rate of inflation fell from 52.3 per cent in 2002 to just 10.5 per cent in 2003, a very notable improvement.[47] But without political stability and security, investors will look askance at locking their money up in projects where the return is uncertain for political reasons. Thus, consolidation of legitimate, institutionalised politics is important not just as a vindication of the political aspirations of Afghans but as an important contributor to legal economic development. This is given a degree of urgency by the growing importance of illegal activities.

The illicit economy

The promotion of human development in Afghanistan is greatly complicated by the position of opium as a significant cash crop. Given the size of the "opium GDP," the sudden elimination of opium would inflict on Afghanistan an economic crash similar to that which set off the Great Depression of 1929. This would be welcomed by the Taliban, but would be disastrous for both long-term stability and long-term counter-narcotics efforts. The opium industry is an extremely complex one, and any measures to deal with it must first come to terms with this complexity.

Opium production has been rising in Afghanistan since the beginning of the 1980s. A detailed World Bank study attributed the rise to changing world market conditions, the collapse of governance, the relationship between drugs and arms, rural pauperisation, comparative advantage, and market development.[48] In 1980, 200 tonnes were produced. By 1990, production had risen to 1600 tonnes. By 1994 it more than doubled again, reaching a total of 3400 tonnes, and in 1999, under the Taliban, it hit an all-time high of 4600 tonnes. This fell to 3300 tonnes in 2000, and in 2001, when the Taliban imposed a ban on cultivation in a last-ditch attempt to win some international support, it plunged to just 185 tonnes. But with the fall of the Taliban cultivation resumed, and had reached 4100 tonnes by 2005.[49] In 2005, the number of people estimated to be involved in opium cultivation was two million. Of the total export value of opium (US$2.7 billion), nearly 80 per cent went in profit to Afghan traffickers; the total "farm-gate" value of opium production was only US$560 million, and the per capita opium income in opium-growing families was US$280.[50] In addition, a 2005 survey concluded that there were 150,000 opium users in Afghanistan, and 50,000 heroin users, out of a total of 920,000 drug users.[51] What these figures do not capture, however, is the variation in production and trading practices and differences in the underlying motivations for cultivation over time and from place to place – and not just between provinces, but within provinces themselves. Opium contributes to livelihoods not just through income from sales, but via wage income and by facilitating access to credit through the *salaam* system, where opium is cultivated in repayment of a prior loan.[52]

The opium trade poses a considerable problem for the Karzai government. Article 7 of the Afghan constitution bans cultivation and smuggling of narcotics, but it is pressure from the wider world that supplies the more relevant constraint. The story of how some drugs (such as opiates) came to be treated by western states as "illicit" while others (such as alcohol and nicotine) were treated as socially acceptable is a labyrinthine one, entangled in the domestic politics of a number of countries.[53] And the control regime to which it has given rise, centred on prohibition of recreational drug use and a "war on drugs," has had numerous perverse consequences, including the generation of super-normal profits for blackmarket suppliers, and the corruption of state instrumentalities in producer countries.[54] These policies create a structure of incentives – namely huge potential profits for traffickers – against which it is extremely difficult for an embryonic state to struggle effectively. At the same time, the Afghan government finds itself under pressure to harmonise its policies with those of the wider world, even though such policies may be of dubious general value, and reflect little sensitivity to the complexities of the opium industry in a country like Afghanistan.

Particular tensions have surrounded the choice of policy instruments to deal with the problem of opium cultivation. One strand of thinking has favoured eradication, perhaps through aerial spraying of crops with a herbicide.[55] Such an approach would run a grave risk of alienating large numbers of Afghans and providing fertile ground for the Taliban to expand their insurgency. For this reason, eradication strategies have been heavily criticised by a number of eminent specialists.[56] The Afghan opium crop is not conveniently concentrated, and this makes comprehensive eradication almost impossible. Furthermore, eradication strategies disregard some basic principles of economics: partial eradication leads to curtailed supply and increased prices, the spectacle of which attracts others to engage in production.[57] A much more rational approach would be to target traffickers, not least because it is they who receive the lion's share of profit from the opium industry. The obstacles to such an approach are political: key traffickers have been allies of the Coalition in the "war on terror," and might well move into spoiler mode if their lucrative activities were disrupted. Afghanistan's new Counter Narcotics Law of December 2005 provides a comprehensive framework for the prosecution of traffickers, but unless the offenders are apprehended, it will remain of largely academic interest. Hitting traffickers is not a hopeless strategy, however, since the trafficking sector is itself fragmented rather than cartelised.[58]

None of this should be read as underestimating the threat posed by the opium industry. Afghanistan is not a narco-state, but it could conceivably become one. But quick fixes will not prevent this from happening; indeed, they could hasten the process. If there is to be a long-term solution, it will be found not in crude eradication or even "crop substitution" but in fostering alternative livelihoods. That said, it is important to recognise that this involves much more than just "crop substitution writ large." The factors that have driven Afghans to cultivate opium are extremely pervasive and deep-rooted, and they will not be uprooted simply by the gift of a short-term income-generating project to a particular district. Rather, it is necessary to rebuild broader institutions of governance and finance so that incentives begin to change. It is equally important to recognise the diverse incentives that drive behaviour, which vary significantly between individuals and go well beyond the strictly economic.[59]

The Afghan state and visions of Afghanistan's economic future

Although the capacities of the Afghan state remain severely limited, the decisions the country's leaders make today can significantly narrow the options they have tomorrow. This is particularly the case in the economic sphere, for Afghanistan is in an increasingly dynamic region, and how it positions itself will affect its future economic prospects. Here, there are a number of models on offer, not necessarily mutually exclusive, for promoting economic well-being and long-term human development prospects. It remains to be seen whether any single one will come to assume a dominant position in the thinking of the government.

One approach would focus on liberating the entrepreneurial capacity of the people themselves. While Afghanistan's poverty means that there is not an obvious surplus of savings on which to draw for local investment, the overall picture may not be quite as dire as this observation would suggest. First, the dysfunctionality of the capital market means that assessing the level of savings within families and communities is not straightforward. Some families, for example, hold savings in cash for use in emergencies. This was the case with some Hazaras from the Jaghori district of Ghazni province,[60] who pooled their savings in order to arrange the escape, through people-smuggling networks, of young men following the Taliban massacres of Hazaras in 1998. Many came by boat to Australia, and despite the efforts of the Australian government to marginalise and exclude them, ultimately became Australian residents.[61] As noted above, the rebuilding of a banking system and capital market offers the prospect that such savings can be invested productively. But a second consideration also should be taken into account. In poor countries, wealth may be locked up in assets that are neither particularly liquid nor – because of uncertainty as to title – capable of being used as security to generate working capital. If capitalism is based on

94

exchangeable private property rights, it is necessary that functioning laws of ownership clarify the location of title so that exchange can occur. As Hernando de Soto has argued in a very influential study, "what the poor are missing are the legally integrated property systems that can convert their work and savings into capital."[62]

A second approach would focus more on Afghanistan's position in a rapidly changing part of the world, identifying new opportunities that would build on its location as a potential bridge between Europe, Central Asia, and South Asia. "Exploiting Afghanistan's position as a land bridge between Central and South Asia, as well as with other economies," argues one writer, "can be a significant source of growth."[63] To the extent that such a strategy is beneficial, it is likely to result from the progressive integration of the Afghan economy into wider regional economies, in the process opening and expanding the markets into which Afghan goods can be sold. Here, it is important to note that despite the disruptions of recent years Afghanistan still has potential exports. These range from obvious commodities and products such as raisins and carpets to less obvious items such as lavender. The accelerating growth of the Indian economy in particular is likely to boost demand for a wide range of imports,[64] although Afghanistan's ability to benefit from this depends very much on a thaw in India–Pakistan relations. This, unfortunately, points to a wider problem with a "bridging" strategy: it depends very much on there being people who wish to use a country as a bridge – which will not necessarily be the case. For example, when the Soviet Union disintegrated at the end of 1991, there was a great deal of speculation about the directions that the new states of Central Asia might take.[65] Some experienced observers expected that Turkey would function as a bridge into this new region of the world, securing influence because many Central Asians spoke Turkic languages. Yet in the years that followed, the new states followed quite diverse political trajectories, including civil war in Tajikistan, heavy-handed authoritarianism in Uzbekistan, and a chilling personality cult in Turkmenistan. Expectations that Turkish influence would grow markedly proved to be misplaced and, especially in the economic sphere, relations with Russia remained very important.[66] Thus, while instability in Afghanistan precluded its acting as a bridge to South Asia, it is far from clear that it would have played such a role even if it had been internally peaceful.

A third approach, a variant of the second, is to use a position as a bridge to extract "rentier" income. To some, the greatest economic opportunity Afghanistan had in recent years arose from oil and gas in neighbouring countries, the notion being that by permitting the transport of such energy resources in pipelines from Turkmenistan, Afghanistan could earn significant rentier income through which reconstruction could be financed. Yet this idea, which flourished during the Taliban period thanks to the activities of the US corporation UNOCAL and the Argentinian firm Bridas, actually highlighted some of the serious difficulties in functioning as a bridge of this sort.[67] A very high level of security is required before lenders will commit significant capital to a project or insurers will provide insurance cover, and security problems persist in many parts of the country. Furthermore, it is doubtful whether such rentier income, which some would regard as simply an example of the so-called "resource curse" in action, necessarily helps a country. In some circumstances, it can erode governmental accountability by giving the state an income source that allows it to ignore the concerns of its people. It can easily fuel patronage rather than reconstruction.

Some forms of state action could contribute to the realisation of a number of these approaches: infrastructural development, particularly the improvement of roads and the electricity grid, can assist private sector development. But that said, some caution is appropriate. If there is a lesson from decades of development experience, it is that no single approach offers a quick-fix solution to Afghanistan's human development challenges. Promoting human development is an extremely complex process. The *Afghanistan National Human Development Report 2004* inadvertently demonstrated this when a chapter entitled "What Kind of Development Vision is Needed for the New Sovereign State?" concluded that

"The role of the Afghan state in the economy should be to ensure economic efficiency, social justice and individual liberty, through an appropriate combination of market intervention and planning."[68] This level of generality avoids a number of profound questions, starting with how one determines what combination of intervention and planning is appropriate, and how one deals with possible tensions among efficiency, justice and liberty.

International assistance

For the foreseeable future, international assistance will be a crucial source of sustenance for the Afghan state. Without the flows of funds that currently support key state activities, they simply would not be discharged; and signs of waning commitment could cause considerable harm to the Karzai regime, even though it also stands to suffer if it is perceived as simply a puppet of the wider world's agendas (as the Shah of Iran discovered to his cost).[69] Nonetheless, there are serious questions to be asked about the effects of such assistance, both economically and politically, and about the implications for Afghan sovereignty of such high levels of dependence. If revenues are not sustainable then a careful judgement must be made about whether the activities that they fund are worth initiating, since the winding-down or withering of projects can leave behind an ugly mess of disappointment and frustration for both implementing staff and beneficiaries. All too many promises to Afghans have not been properly honoured, and in some ways it is better not to make promises at all than to make them and subsequently break them.[70]

As mentioned in the previous chapter, the initial approach to reconstruction was one of "lead nation" responsibility for activities in particular sectors. This was an approach that I, for one, had supported in the early 1990s to overcome the problems that can arise when, as Fazel Haq Saikal and I wrote at the time, "the connection between the contribution of a particular donor and the success or failure of a particular project is too tenuous for any sense of donor responsibility to develop."[71] In post-Taliban Afghanistan, however, this method has given rise to three problems. One is that if donors' approaches are flawed, an entire sector can misfire, with no obvious corrective mechanism positioned to come into play. A second problem, equally if not more serious, is that the Afghan government may receive relatively little credit for success. Instead of being a frontline agent whose achievements Afghans may feel deserve some reward, it becomes yet another passive observer of the development process. Third, local capacity-building may be devalued in favour of the employment of external implementers; this can often generate a quick impact, but leaves long-term challenges unaddressed.

International support for Afghanistan has been voiced on a number of occasions, notably at major international conferences in Tokyo on 21–22 January 2002, in Berlin on 31 March–1 April 2004, and in London in 2006. At these conferences the Afghan government presented or foreshadowed detailed analyses of key areas for which funding was required – principally its 2002 *National Development Framework*; a report entitled *Securing Afghanistan's Future* prepared for the 2004 conference; and an updated and expanded *Afghanistan National Development Strategy* circulated before the 2006 meeting. The political reality, however, was and is that donor priorities and the Afghan government's priorities do not necessarily coincide. Donors, at least in theory, are accountable to their own publics and to auditing agencies which examine how monies have been spent, and this can lead to a chain of payments that bypasses the Afghan government and instead funds agencies, consulting firms, not-for-profit agencies and private corporations domiciled in the donor state. This has been particularly a problem with funds from the United States, which has been the largest single donor. In addition, the political imperative to deliver rapid results has on occasion operated at the expense of both quality and sustainability. In 2002–03, less than a quarter of spending by US agencies was on longer-term reconstruction needs.[72] In late 2005, reports began to surface of shoddy workmanship, inadequate oversight, and waste in the implementation of key programs funded by the US Agency for International Development – programs which had been fast-tracked in preparation for Afghanistan's 2004 presidential election.[73] This fast-tracking, ironically, came after two years of slow movement on the aid front more generally, and possibly in reaction to it: while US$5.37 billion in total had been committed to Afghanistan by November 2003, the value of projects actually completed was only US$112.5 million.[74]

Beyond governments are two other kinds of actor: international organisations and their associated specialised and humanitarian agencies; and non-state actors such as private contractors and not-for-profit agencies. The UN system, of course, has been very heavily involved in Afghanistan from the moment of the Taliban regime's overthrow, and despite its avowed adoption of a "light footprint" approach, which I discuss in more detail in the next chapter, it has been a significant source of both material resources and expertise. Other international agencies have also been heavily involved, including the Bretton Woods institutions (especially the World Bank), the Asian Development Bank, and a number of offices associated with pan-European institutions, notably the European Union and the European Commission.

Much more controversial have been private contractors and non-government organisations. Private contractors, employed for their technical expertise, have absorbed many millions of dollars, although exact amounts are very difficult to determine. Contractors' remunerations tend to be large even by western standards, and astronomical from an Afghan's perspective. There have been very few evaluations of how frequently they have delivered value for money, and how lasting their impact has been, but a 2006 CorpWatch report identified some alarming cases of waste, mismanagement, and profligacy.[75] Any comprehensive evaluation would need also to take account of the resentment that the behaviour of at least some contractors has caused, for while many have been cautious and responsible, others have been reckless in their personal behaviour, contributing to a growing sex industry in Kabul which many ordinary Afghans find not only offensive, but also deeply threatening to their sense of ownership of what they see as their personal space.[76]

Non-government organisations, or NGOs, come in many forms, including long-established and reputable agencies with strong track records of work in Afghanistan, newer foreign or international NGOs seeking to work in a fast-changing environment, and a growing number of Afghan NGOs. Some fly-by-night organisations, both Afghan and foreign, have sought to do well by doing good. In 2004 and 2005, NGOs came under strong attack from Dr Ramazan Bachardoust, a populist former planning minister who secured election to the Wolesi Jirga from the province of Kabul.[77] His scattergun criticisms, routinely blurring the distinction between NGOs and contractors and between different types of NGOs, were pitched directly to those Afghans concerned that not enough was improving in their daily lives. While his attacks did highlight the importance of developing a clearer framework for NGO operations, they also threatened to damage a number of agencies that had done more than Bachardoust ever had to assist ordinary Afghans to survive in desperate circumstances.

The question of who will really occupy the driver's seat in Afghanistan remains unresolved. Formal sovereignty resides in the Karzai government, but with three-quarters of "state-like" expenditure beyond its control it clearly faces real problems in realising its objectives. In the past, strategic coordination in Afghanistan and elsewhere has been debated in the context of relations between different parts of the UN system, or between the UN and NGOs. Some have favoured an apolitical autonomous or semi-autonomous "humanitarian space" in which principles prevail,[78] while others have argued, in the words of the essayist David Rieff, that "what Afghanistan demonstrated was that humanitarianism was too important a matter to be left to humanitarians alone."[79] One thing is clear: at some point, if Afghanistan's transition is to be meaningful, it will need to take over decision-making in areas currently closed to it. This, however, will depend on the broader evolution of its relations with the wider world. It is to this topic that the next chapter turns.

CHAPTER 5

Afghanistan and the world

Afghanistan is not the isolated mountain kingdom that it might once have seemed to casual outside observers; rather, it is connected to the world by complex considerations of cultural affinity, geopolitics, the regional tensions of Southwest Asia, economic ties and ideology, as well as its new relationship with the United States. It requires great dexterity and delicacy to maintain a position as a pro-American Muslim state without becoming entangled in such sources of trouble as the US–Iran relationship, the backwash from the March 2003 US invasion of Iraq, and the Arab–Israeli dispute. A similar degree of dexterity is needed to avoid a domestic backlash from the relationship with the Bush administration, which many Muslims have come, rightly or wrongly, to see as hostile to Islam. It is therefore appropriate to open this chapter with a more detailed discussion of the US–Afghanistan relationship.

Afghanistan and the United States

The United States is the principal guarantor of Afghanistan's transition, indeed its linchpin, since a number of the other governments contributing assistance are driven not so much by intrinsic concern for Afghanistan as by a desire to consolidate their own relations with the United States. In addition, by committing support to Afghanistan, states friendly with the US can insulate themselves from pressure to contribute to ongoing Coalition operations in Iraq, which are no less perilous than those in Afghanistan and likely to be more contentious domestically. Thus, any waning of US interest or commitment could have wider flow-on effects, in the medium if not the short term, about which Afghans should rightly feel alarm. The risk of total abandonment is quite low. America's commitment has been uncontroversial domestically and internationally,[1] just as its support for the Mujahideen was in the 1980s. Then, the struggle of the Afghans was rightly perceived as defensive, and US support for it as appropriate per se, as well as in the wider context of Soviet–American relations. Now, support for transition in Afghanistan is also rightly perceived as defensive, in the light of the assault on the United States of September 2001 initiated by terrorists operating from Afghan territory. This sets Afghanistan apart from Iraq, where the recent combat has been a war of choice rather than of necessity. The Afghanistan commitment has been far less costly in human terms for America: as of late April 2006, the total number of US deaths in Afghanistan and its immediate vicinity as a result of hostile action following the 2001 intervention was 141,[2] barely 5 per cent of the total US deaths in Iraq from March 2003. Therefore, the immediate "worst-case" scenario for the Karzai government is not the almost total abandonment of the 1990s, which I discussed in chapter one, but rather a phasing down of commitment, leaving the government protected for the moment in Kabul and to a lesser extent in other cities, but weak in the countryside.

The US relationship with Kabul has passed through several phases since the Bonn agreement was signed, and these are largely associated with the varying approaches of different US ambassadors. From March 2002 to November 2003, Ambassador Robert P. Finn, a distinguished career diplomat with great experience in Central and West Asia, headed the embassy, bringing a resident US ambassador to Kabul for the first time since the killing of Ambassador Adolph Dubs in 1979. His term was marked by the shift from interim to transitional administration in June 2002. Finn had to cope with the presence of a special envoy of the US president, Dr Zalmay Khalilzad, who was of Afghan birth but had lived in the United States for many years and obtained a PhD at the University of Chicago. Khalilzad succeeded Dr Finn as ambassador in November 2003 and served until 2005. He was a very different kind of ambassador, maintaining constant contact with Karzai and not hesitating to intervene in Afghan political discussions. This was a quite deliberate approach on his part. In a later reflection on his experiences, he argued that "Intensive political and diplomatic engagement with national leaders is needed to craft a national compact among competing groups and to form a partnership to execute a mutually agreed strategy for reconstruction."[3] This had its advantages and disadvantages. On the one hand, thanks to his linguistic skills and long familiarity with Afghanistan, he was able to hit the ground running. On the other hand, as a person of Afghan origin, he was vulnerable to being accused, whether fairly or not, of seeking to advantage some groups over others on grounds of ethnicity. (This is a charge to which any US ambassador posted to the country from which he originates is likely to be subject if that country is internally fractured.) In 2005, upon his appointment as US ambassador to Iraq, Khalilzad was succeeded in Kabul by Ambassador Ronald E. Neumann, a career diplomat whose father had been US ambassador to Afghanistan from 1966 to 1973. Ambassador Neumann pursued a lower-key approach to Afghan politicking than his immediate predecessor had done. The ambassadors' work has been well complemented by the US generals who have commanded Coalition forces in Afghanistan, particularly Lieutenant-General Karl W. Eikenberry, a graduate of West Point, Harvard, and Stanford who took over command on 3 May 2005, and who has been extremely alert to the need to recognise the long-term as well as short-term effects of military action.[4]

Of all the issues in the bilateral relationship, none is potentially more sensitive than the question of future permanent basing rights for US forces in the region. At present, as noted in chapter three, there is still a widespread disposition to accept US forces in Afghanistan. This, however, is on the understanding that their presence will not be permanent and colonialist in character, and even then, to some degree, the presence of US forces has led parts of the population to view Karzai as a puppet of Washington. As a result, both US and Afghan spokesmen have been careful in their choice of language when seeking to define the parameters of a longer term relationship. In April 2005, during a visit to Afghanistan by US Secretary of Defense Donald H. Rumsfeld, Karzai spoke of a "sustained economic and political relationship and most importantly of all, a strategic security relationship to help Afghanistan defend itself."[5] These priorities were reflected in the Joint Declaration of the United States–Afghanistan Strategic Partnership released on 23 May 2005, which stated that "U.S. military forces operating in Afghanistan will continue to have access to Bagram Air Base and its facilities, and facilities at other locations as may be mutually determined and that the U.S. and Coalition forces are to continue to have the freedom of action required to conduct appropriate military operations based on consultations and pre-agreed procedures."[6] The country that could obviously feel threatened by close military ties between Afghanistan and the United States is Iran, but it has actually reacted with relative calm to the deployment next door of US forces, since it had its own severe differences with the Taliban and with Sunni extremism more generally.[7] But that said, any movement towards permanent basing would likely be read in Teheran as part of an expanding anti-Iran strategy, and could lead to a much less constructive Iranian approach to the Afghan situation. Afghanistan's caution about its long-term relationship with the United States is well-founded, since it has to live with its own region as well.

Another issue with the potential to cause friction and possibly worse is the conduct of US troops in the field and in places where prisoners are held. Thus far Afghanistan has not witnessed a crisis comparable to the Abu Ghraib prisoner abuse scandal in Iraq,[8] but there have been some serious cases of brutality towards individuals in detention[9] and a number of deaths have resulted, with very little indication that the perpetrators have much to fear from the US military justice system. A 2006 report by US human rights organisations claimed that "at least sixty cases" have occurred in Afghanistan "in which U.S. military and civilian personnel are alleged to have abused detainees."[10] The political perils associated with abuses of this sort should not be underrated, and no comfort should be taken from the fact that so far there has been no explosion in response to what has occurred. For about a week from 11 May 2005, serious disturbances occurred in Jalalabad, Kabul and elsewhere in Afghanistan after *Newsweek* magazine published a report, later retracted, of desecration of the Koran at the Guantanamo Bay detention facility. Twenty people were killed, hundreds were injured, and a great deal of property damage occurred, especially to offices of foreign organisations. The same could happen on a larger scale if a major prisoner abuse scandal blew up in Afghanistan itself. Karzai's Taliban opponents could hardly wish for more.

The central difficulty for Karzai is that in seeking to combat such abuse he carries relatively little weight. US military personnel in facilities such as the Bagram base north of Kabul are not subject to his control, and his occasional expressions of concern have had a muted tone, which has probably done him more harm than good. Yet the problem is potentially grave. Robert Cryer has argued that the "way our friends act also reflects upon us, and thus it is important to take care when choosing friends and allies, and appraise the actions of both friend and foe by reference to the same law."[11] Cryer was writing of the United States' relationship with elements of the anti-Taliban "Northern Alliance," but the same argument applies equally to Karzai's relationship with the United States. Even in relation to illegal roadblocks established by the United States in downtown Kabul, an issue taken up with gusto by members of the new Wolesi Jirga, the limits of the president's influence have been all too clear. If the United States continues to take Karzai for granted, it may one day discover that it has gone too far.

Afghanistan and Southwest Asia

The greatest challenge Afghanistan faces in its region emanates from Pakistan, in the ways detailed in chapter three. Relations have long been fraught with difficulty,[12] and Pakistan's hostility to Pushtun nationalism and its long-term interest in dominating a compliant Afghanistan are entrenched features of the regional political landscape. But there is more texture to Pakistan's position than such a terse account suggests. For years its leaders have believed that Pakistan's role as a frontline state during the Soviet–Afghan war and its decades of hospitality to Afghan refugees (several million of whom still live in Pakistan) should give it a say in who should rule Afghanistan. Few Afghans believe it should have any such say. While Pakistan was put in a very awkward position by Washington's demand in 2001 that it declare itself either friend or foe, it actually has a significant interest in the continuation of the "War on Terror," rather than its concluding with the capture of Osama Bin Laden. Pakistan can at least claim a significant role in the "War on Terror," just as it did during the anti-Soviet struggle of the 1980s. Without such a factor at play, the United States is likely to give increasing weight to its relationship with India, a threshold great power with much to offer the United States in terms of trade and the supply of human capital. Pakistan has struggled over decades with the ambivalence of its relationship with the United States,[13] and more recently has had the distressing experience of visits by successive US presidents, Clinton in March 2000 and Bush in March 2006, which almost amounted to studied insults to Pakistan when compared with the warmth lavished on India.

By any measure, Pakistan is a deeply troubled state.[14] Arguably, it poses a greater threat to global security than Iraq ever did, although for rather different reasons. It is the most likely candidate to become a nuclear-armed failed state. Pakistan has suffered enormously from the fragility of its domestic institutions, as well as from an existential sense of insecurity which the loss of East Pakistan certainly fuelled.[15] In spawning the Taliban, its leadership of the mid 1990s truly played with fire, given the real risk that the Taliban or something like them would wash back into conservative parts of Pakistan such as Baluchistan or the Northwest Frontier Province.[16] President Pervez Musharraf, who took power in a military coup in October 1999, is personally more liberal than were a number of his senior military colleagues, and for that reason has been publicly treated with considerable respect by the Bush administration and other western leaders. And since the election of Dr

Manmohan Singh as India's prime minister there has also been something of a thaw in India–Pakistan relations, building on early progress during the premiership of Atal Bihari Vajpayee. Yet on Afghanistan, Musharraf has proved unable to move beyond the mindset of superordination that has crippled Pakistan's relationship with its poor but proud western neighbour for so long. Afghanistan's leadership is now convinced that Pakistan is up to its old tricks, and Afghan officials are well placed to argue this case to Washington.

Unless and until Pakistan addresses its own problems of internal political order and tension with India, it is unlikely that it will function as a constructive actor in the region. "Democratisation" is much more a matter of reconfiguring institutional relationships than of holding elections. Pakistan has a long history of corrupted voting, and as long as the military is positioned to intervene in politics with relative ease, the cream of Pakistan's civilians will opt for either business careers or emigration. Improved relations with India would cut away some of the rationale for the special guardianship role the Pakistan military purports to play, so major power diplomacy may be useful in promoting a healthier climate on the subcontinent, particularly in relation to Kashmir. This is not for a moment to suggest that there are easy or obvious solutions for a problem of this complexity, but rather to suggest that the need for an active approach to its resolution is urgent.[17]

While the regional relationship with Pakistan is the most awkward for Afghanistan to manage, there is some risk that its relationship with Iran could also be complicated by exogenous factors. The tensions between the United States and Iran over Iran's nuclear energy programs, compounded by the 2005 election of the hardline populist Mahmoud Ahmadinejad as Iran's president, threaten Afghanistan indirectly. Any US air strike at its nuclear facilities could tempt Iran to stir up trouble in countries such as Iraq and Afghanistan where there are significant concentrations of US troops, and regimes that enjoy US backing and could function as surrogate targets if US forces proved too difficult to hit. The Karzai government has been careful to nurture its own relationship with Iran, and

Iran has hitherto been a cooperative and constructive actor in Afghanistan,[18] but an angry Iranian regime could easily find unofficial channels through which to pursue a spoiler campaign. Unfortunately, the US approach to Iran has long been complicated by problems of distance, misperception, and emotion, which have also at times characterised the approach of Iranian political leaders to Washington. It is a matter of considerable regret that during the presidency of the moderate Muhammad Khatami, the United States retained such a distant posture, epitomised by President Bush's description of Iran in his January 2002 State of the Union address as part of an "axis of evil." This played straight into the hands of hard-line populists.[19]

Afghanistan's relations with India are cordial, but this significantly complicates relations with Pakistan. Until the end of the 1970s, dealings between India and Afghanistan were warm, especially when relations between Pakistan and Afghanistan were chilly. In 1980, following the Soviet invasion, the Indian government of Indira Gandhi opted to take a broadly pro-Soviet position at the UN General Assembly Emergency Special Session on Afghanistan.[20] This persisted, although with various nuances, until the collapse of the communist regime in 1992, and was driven by a mixture of fidelity to the Soviet Union and hostility to Pakistan as a supporter of the Afghan resistance. Thereafter, India moved to improve its relations with the Rabbani government, and throughout the Taliban period the Afghan embassy in New Delhi was under the control of anti-Taliban forces; Massoud Khalili, the Afghan ambassador to India, was severely injured in the bomb blast that killed Ahmad Shah Massoud. While there was a brief flurry of concern in December 1999 that India might modify its position, triggered by some remarks made by the Indian external affairs minister Jaswant Singh after he had flown to Kandahar to bring home the Indian victims of an aircraft hijacking,[21] nothing of the sort eventuated. Since the overthrow of the Taliban, India has been active diplomatically in Afghanistan, posting very accomplished diplomats to Kabul, with the most recent appointee, Ambassador Rakesh Sood, having previously held a senior position in the Indian embassy in Washington.

This Indian influence is, of course, resented by Pakistan, and has spawned wild claims that Indian consulates in Afghanistan are being used to support separatism in Baluchistan. The fact that President Karzai was educated in India, where he completed an MA at the University of Himachal Pradesh in Shimla, only adds to Pakistan's paranoia. It would be in the interests of both India and Afghanistan to ensure that their relationship develops discreetly, if only to ensure that Indian contractors in Afghanistan, of whom there are now many, are not further singled out for Taliban attack.

Afghanistan and the United Nations

In conflict and post-conflict situations, it is often elements of the UN system that provide some degree of continuous international presence. Afghanistan has been a UN member since 1946, and an Afghan diplomat, Abdul Rahman Pazhwak, was president of the UN General Assembly in 1966. Through political missions, humanitarian agencies, and the attention of high UN organs such as the Security Council and the General Assembly, the United Nations has had an extensive history of involvement in Afghanistan since 1980.[22] Given its salience as a source of political legitimacy, it was virtually inevitable that the task of helping to craft new political arrangements for post-Taliban Afghanistan would fall to it. But this was only the beginning of a much wider involvement, which saw the establishment of a significant UN mission in Afghanistan and extensive activity by UN agencies in reconstruction and relief. In the period 2001–03, 45.9 per cent of assistance to Afghanistan was provided through the United Nations and its agencies, compared with 27.8 per cent provided directly to government, 16.5 per cent through private companies, and 9.7 per cent through non-government organisations.[23]

The most important figure in shaping the United Nations' contribution to Afghanistan was Ambassador Lakhdar Brahimi of Algeria, the UN under-secretary-general for special assignments. He began his political career in the 1950s as a representative in Southeast Asia of the Algerian independence movement, and he served as Algerian foreign minister before moving to the United

Nations. He worked cooperatively with the United States in Haiti, and headed the United Nations Observer Mission in South Africa at the time of the 1994 election. He had served as special envoy for Afghanistan from 28 July 1997 to 20 October 1999, but suspended his mediation given the lack of scope for progress. On 3 October 2001, UN Secretary-General Kofi Annan appointed Brahimi as his special representative with a "widened mandate entailing overall authority for the humanitarian and political endeavours of the United Nations in Afghanistan."[24] In between, Brahimi had headed a high-level UN panel which had strongly recommended (in the so-called "Brahimi Report") that mandates for UN missions reflect the realities of available resources.[25] This very much shaped his approach to the UN's new mandate for Afghanistan. The United Nations Assistance Mission in Afghanistan, or UNAMA, established by Security Council Resolution 1401 of 28 March 2002, followed a model outlined in a March 2002 report by the secretary-general. The report recommended that "The overall objective of UNAMA should be to provide support for the implementation of the Bonn Agreement processes, including the stabilization of the emerging structures of the Afghan Interim Authority, while recognizing that the responsibility for the Agreement's implementation ultimately rests with the Afghans themselves." It stated that "UNAMA should undertake close coordination and consultation with the Afghan Interim Authority and other Afghan actors to ensure that Afghan priorities lead the mission's assistance efforts." And it concluded that "UNAMA should aim to bolster Afghan capacity (both official and non-governmental), relying on as limited an international presence and on as many Afghan staff as possible, and using common support services where possible, thereby leaving a light expatriate 'footprint'."[26] Brahimi headed UNAMA until shortly after his 70th birthday in early 2004, when he was succeeded by one of his deputies, Jean Arnault of France; he, in turn, was succeeded in early 2006 by Tom Koenigs of Germany.

The "light footprint" approach was adopted partly in recognition of the distinctive character of the Afghanistan mission. As the political scientist Richard Caplan put it, UNAMA is "an assistance mission with no operational responsibility for administering any part of Afghanistan."[27] In that respect, it differs radically from UN missions in countries and territories such as Cambodia, Eastern Slavonia, Bosnia and Herzegovina, Kosovo, and East Timor. The approach has certainly had its critics. One strand finds the notion of a "light footprint" insufficiently precise: "It seems that every agency is at liberty to determine what 'light' should mean for itself, and also what 'light' should mean for others, apparently, with no requirement that the criteria should be universal."[28] Others argue that despite Brahimi's best efforts, the footprint was not as "light" as he had intended, and there is no doubt that the arcane regulations which govern the operation of the UN system have on occasion obstructed local capacity-building efforts. According to a third strand of criticism, the mission's footprint has been too light: Chris Johnson and Jolyon Leslie, for example, argue that "the notion of 'Afghan ownership' has over time been used as an excuse for the UN and other international players to abdicate their responsibility in the face of the more difficult issues of the transition. Nowhere was this more apparent than on the issue of human rights, and specifically transitional justice."[29] This is a complex issue, which I will discuss in more detail in the final chapter.

What deserves to be reiterated is the realism of Brahimi's approach to conducting a mission of this sort. Afghanistan had an active political class, not eager to be pushed aside to make way for instruments of international governance. This militated in favour of an assistance mission rather than anything more intrusive. Furthermore, Brahimi wanted to avoid the United Nations' becoming a surrogate state (although the emergence of the "second civil service" phenomenon might raise questions about how successfully this laudable objective was realised). Finally, a smaller, sustainable mission has more to offer than a grandiose mission that lacks the resources to realise its goals. The proponents of a "light footprint" approach were guided by a level-headed sense of what "international society" was likely to deliver, and by a recognition that little good would be served by raising local expectations to unsustainable levels.[30] Keeping a mission "light" can be a constant struggle, however, in which capacity-building is under threat from pressures to deliver quick results. This came to a head in the area of electoral assistance, not a direct UNAMA task, but certainly a key responsibility of the UN system in tandem with specially designed Afghan institutions. In preparation for the 2004 presidential election, a great deal of attention was given to developing local capacity, partly because the experienced international staff who were involved in the process recognised that exposing younger Afghans to the mechanics of running a clean election was something good in itself. In 2005, by contrast, local capacity-building received a lower priority, in part because of the greater complexity of the electoral processes, and international staff played concomitantly greater roles. The issues of who will run Afghanistan's next elections, and who will pay for them, remain substantially unresolved. That said, UNAMA is by now a well-established actor on the Afghan landscape, and is likely to remain one for the foreseeable future, although perhaps without quite the standing that Brahimi's unique skills and experience gave it.

Afghanistan and "globalised Islam"

If links to the United Nations give Afghanistan one kind of international connection, its entanglements with globalised Islam offer another, albeit very different in character. Globalisation has provided means for social groups to build networks across international boundaries on an unprecedented scale, and while much of this activity is either positive or innocuous, on occasion it can have a dark side. One example is the development of transnational Islamic radicalism, from which Afghanistan has not been immune, and which may well continue to be a disruptive influence on its society and politics. In preaching the significance of a transnational community of believers (*ummah*), Islamists challenge to some degree the axioms upon which the Westphalian system of sovereign states is based, although in both Islamic and western thought the picture is much more complicated than such a simple dichotomy might lead one to expect.[31] Transnational

Islamic radicalism is a manifestation of the transformational effects of globalisation, which both detaches people from traditional ways of thinking and behaving, and connects them to others who are equally disoriented. While Muslim radicals propound various highly contestable ideas about the Islamic faith,[32] they also have a range of concrete political concerns, of which the situation in Afghanistan is only one, and probably not the most important when compared with the Arab–Israeli dispute and the war in Iraq. Nonetheless, it is an area of concern, routinely cited by Osama Bin Laden and Aiman al-Zawahiri in the audio and video tapes they release to the Qatar-based television network Al Jazeera; and disarray in Afghanistan is in their interests, since it would reflect poorly on the United States as the principal sponsor of transition. In a narrowly military sense, Afghanistan is not of especial importance to radical Islamists, whose disposition to think strategically can be overestimated.[33] But in a symbolic sense, it is enormously important: it is the country in which, from the Islamists' perspective, it was established that a superpower could be defeated on the battlefield, and it was also the initial theatre of operations for President Bush's "War on Terror."

The scale of the internal threat in Afghanistan can be judged by reference to the assassination of Ahmad Shah Massoud on 9 September 2001. This offered a very interesting window into the mindset of Islamic radicalism, since the target of the killing was neither a westerner nor a recipient of significant western assistance, although he was popular in some European circles and in one of his few trips outside Afghanistan had visited Paris and Strasbourg on 4–7 April 2001. Massoud was by all accounts a devout and pious Muslim, but had long been bitterly opposed by radicals such as the Hezb-e Islami's Gulbuddin Hekmatyar; on the eve of the collapse of the communist regime in April 1992, his spokesman had candidly stated that "Hekmatyar can't agree to anything that includes Ahmed Shah Masoud."[34] While this was partly a manifestation of personal jealousy, it also reflected the tension between radical Islamists and more moderate pro-western Muslim leaders, of which Massoud was an example. A figure such as Karzai is equally at risk, and he and his key ministers and advisers need to be very careful about their personal security. There are many Islamist radicals who see Muslim countries, rather than western states, as the central battlefields on which their struggles will be played out, and regard direct attacks on civilians in western countries as totally counter-productive.[35] This is not, however, a position from which rulers such as President Karzai can derive much joy.

How should the Afghan government position itself vis-à-vis these forces and groups? Here, of course, it is necessary to distinguish transnational groups such as al-Qaeda from transnational groups such as the Taliban. The former are capable of engaging in a campaign of assassination and may be able to fund further terrorism, but are hardly an existential threat to Afghanistan (any more than they are an existential threat to any western government). Furthermore, under US pressure Pakistan has moved against al-Qaeda, and President Musharraf has been the subject of a number of attempted assassinations as a result. The Taliban pose a different order of threat. They are not under pressure from Pakistan, and are driven by a burning resentment of Karzai and his associates, whom they blame for their own demise as a regime. One answer to the question of how the Afghan government should position itself might be that it should seek to engage with "moderate" elements from within hitherto threatening groups. Karzai, for example, has made occasional statements indicating a willingness to accept "moderate Taliban" as participants in political life, and the Taliban's former "foreign minister," Wakil Ahmad Muttawakil, even ran (unsuccessfully) as a candidate for the Wolesi Jirga in 2005, publishing a short memoir as part of his campaign. This approach, however, has not much to offer as a general political strategy, since it disturbs moderate non-Pushtuns without doing anything to blunt the operations of the Taliban leaders from their bases in Pakistan. A more plausible, although less comforting, answer is that there is no easy answer, and that the most the government can seek to do is deliver good governance at the local level in order to deny the Taliban oxygen, as well as lobby the United States to put more pressure on Pakistan to shut down the Taliban's bases. But that said, Karzai should avoid going out of his way to support the United States on issues where Afghanistan's own vital interests are not engaged. Adopting a reflexively pro-American position is akin to bungee jumping when one does not know the length of the rope.

Protecting Afghanistan in a troubled region

Afghanistan's strategic situation is an awkward one, and there are no prospects for immediate relief. It is fundamentally disadvantaged by being a landlocked state, and its tense relations with Pakistan have aggravated this problem. When diplomatic relations between Afghanistan and Pakistan were severed between 1961 and 1963, Afghanistan suffered the greater harm, and this was one of the factors that contributed to the replacement of Muhammad Daoud as prime minister and the inauguration of the era of "New Democracy." Clearly one option Afghanistan can pursue is to seek great and powerful friends from beyond the region in order to offset some of the pressures regional states might bring to bear upon it. As noted in chapter one, Afghanistan historically combined a formal posture of non-alignment (*bi tarafi*) with a search for such friends, and it was dusty indifference on the part of the United States that in part saw Daoud draw dangerously close to the Soviet Union in the 1950s.[36] The idea that Afghanistan is a non-aligned state is quite deeply ingrained in popular thinking, and certainly reinforces Afghans' robust sense of independence. Thus, a real challenge for Afghan leaders is to find ways of exploiting the benefits of alignment without actually appearing to do so.

The starting point for an assessment of how best to protect Afghanistan is to recognise that Afghanistan is unlikely ever itself to be strong enough to deter meddling by neighbours such as Pakistan and Iran, and would be imprudent to rely on great powers to honour their rhetorical commitments to stand by Afghanistan in the long run. For these reasons, Afghanistan has a very strong interest in promoting comprehensive solutions to the interlocking regional security dilemmas that make its position so difficult. The most important of these is the tension between India and Pakistan. While Pakistan's compulsive drive to dominate Afghanistan has much to do with its bitter memories of the Pushtunistan dispute, it also derives from a fear of being threatened on two fronts, from India to the east and from an unsympathetic and possibly pro-Indian Afghanistan to the west. During the Taliban period, it was also convenient for Pakistan to have Kashmiri militants trained in camps in Afghanistan, off the territory of Pakistan itself. No other state would gain more from a genuine and lasting improvement in India–Pakistan relations than Afghanistan. Promoting such an improvement would be a useful step for Afghanistan to take, although it is not much in the mood to do so and would not likely have much effect unless its approach were strongly reinforced by Washington and other major capitals. Perhaps fortunately, the 1998 nuclear tests carried out by India and then Pakistan virtually ensure ongoing major power interest in the stability of the subcontinent. To the extent that they contribute to a relationship of stable deterrence between India and Pakistan[37] the tests may also have created political space for intractable problems to receive some attention, although progress is likely to be slow given the decades of scepticism and distrust.

That said, it would make sense for Afghanistan to review some of its own old positions. Its regional relations have suffered nothing but harm from its entanglement with the idea of Pushtunistan, which is by now an utterly hopeless cause, and there is great force in Barnett R. Rubin's recent observation that "Islamabad will not respect a border that Kabul does not recognize."[38] As Rubin goes on to note, this is domestically a very sensitive issue, and stirring up the tribes of Pakistan has long been a tactic employed by Afghan rulers when they have wanted to fire a shot across Pakistan's bows.[39] But the breakdown of the Afghan state and the weakening of its borders long ago turned the tables, making Afghanistan far more vulnerable to Pakistani manipulation of forces within Afghanistan. Were Afghanistan to accept the Durand Line as a permanent border, this would be a striking confidence-building measure as far as Pakistan is concerned. The risk to President Karzai, of course, derives from domestic politics. Against all considerations of practicality, there are still Pushtun chauvinists in Afghanistan who regard Peshawar as a part of "Pushtunistan" to be liberated, and it would therefore require a carefully negotiated elite consensus to protect a ruler who chose to set out a new position on this issue.

What Southwest Asia has notably lacked has been any effective architecture for the promotion of cooperative security. The South Asian Association for Regional Cooperation, which Afghanistan has moved to join, has been notoriously ineffectual, although the blame for this largely lies with its tempestuous members rather than with the association itself. But this is not to say that enhancing regional organisation is beyond the realms of possibility. Effective security architectures not only reflect improving relations between states; they can actually enhance and consolidate positive moves by providing channels through which lingering problems can be confronted. They are often multi-layered: in Southeast Asia, for example, the Association of Southeast Asian Nations is complemented by the ASEAN Regional Forum and the Council for Security Cooperation in the Asia-Pacific, a "second-track diplomacy" channel through which complex issues can be canvassed without the existing positions of states being compromised. An attempt to institutionalise second-track contacts in Southwest Asia, perhaps starting with Iran, Afghanistan, Pakistan, and India, could be a positive and creative first step.

In the previous chapter, I discussed the model of Afghanistan as an economic bridge between South and Central Asia. It might also be possible for Afghanistan to position itself as a political bridge in its region. Its historical experiences of this kind have been limited, although in an unexpected move in May 1995, the Rabbani government hosted direct talks between the president of Tajikistan, Imamali Rakhmanov, and the leader of the Islamic opposition in Tajikistan, Said Abdullah Nuri. In certain circumstances, Afghanistan might be able to function as an honest broker between different regional forces, not because it is strong but because it is weak. Nonetheless, to do so would require considerable diplomatic dexterity.

Reintegrating Afghanistan as a normal state

While Afghanistan's foreign policy is in part concerned with positioning itself in the world, it is also concerned with the country's own identity. In recent decades, Afghanistan has enjoyed the unhappy status of either pariah state or failed state. In the long run, it would benefit greatly from becoming what one might loosely call a "normal" state. A "normal" state enjoys reasonably high levels of juridical and empirical sovereignty with legitimate forms of internal authority, and relates to other states as a sovereign equal, even though inequalities of power are of course endemic in the international system.

Just as individuals live in many social worlds, countries too can seek to manage a multiplicity of identifications, although domestic political factors will likely shape the salience that different identifications receive. Here, Afghanistan faces a range of important choices: region, political values, and culture can drive it in subtly different directions. Considerations of regionalism could prompt a foreign policy focused predominantly on managing relations with neighbours, and there is no doubt that in any circumstances this will be an important element of Afghan foreign policy. Political values are also a factor of considerable importance. With the exception of Gulbuddin Hekmatyar, ironically the principal beneficiary of US-funded aid to the Mujahideen in the 1980s, there have been few virulently anti-western voices in Afghanistan, and Afghans are certainly not hostile to democracy as a political device: the turnout at the 2004 presidential election made that clear. Figures such as Ahmad Shah Massoud were consistently eager to win the backing of key western states, and it was a tragedy that the United States, swayed by the influence of Pakistan, long failed to recognise the possibility of working cooperatively with a moderate Islamist of Massoud's ilk. And Karzai and some of his key ministers have spent a great deal of time in the United States and other western countries, and in most cases were well integrated and successful in their new lives in the west when the opportunity to return to Afghanistan emerged.

But Afghanistan is also a predominantly Muslim country, and this cultural factor limits what a country like the United States might reasonably expect of Afghanistan in its foreign policy orientation. The most important of these limitations relates to the politics of the wider Middle East. Afghanistan has historically not been heavily involved in the Arab–Israeli dispute, but its orientation has been broadly pro-Palestinian. In the United States, by contrast, there are strong pro-Israel lobbies, whose political strength has been the subject of lively recent discussion.[40] It would be deeply unfortunate if the United States sought to pressure Afghanistan to take any kind of stand at odds with its longstanding orientation on this issue. But more broadly, President Karzai runs the risk of being drawn needlessly into discussion of issues that simply expose tensions between cultural and political values. Thus, when Karzai was pressed during a European visit to comment on sacrilegious cartoons in a Danish newspaper, he found himself in an impossible position, where any response he gave would cause offence to some constituency that it would not benefit Afghanistan to alienate. It is easy to view President Karzai as an archetype of a modern moderate Muslim, but to press him to confirm these credentials does him no favour at all.

CHAPTER 6

Whither Afghanistan?

In early 2006, the annual Failed States Index was published in the influential magazine *Foreign Policy*.[1] The countries analysed were classed as either "critical," "in danger," or "borderline." Despite years of international effort, Afghanistan remained squarely in the "critical" category, ahead (at tenth position on the list) of notorious trouble spots such as Liberia, Burundi, and Sierra Leone. While Afghans could take some comfort from the fact that Afghanistan was not rated as poorly as Iraq, clearly their country still faces huge difficulties that make its future trajectory very hard to predict. In this chapter, I draw together some reflections on the tendencies, both positive and negative, that are currently at work in Afghanistan, and suggest that extreme vigilance is required if the country's problems are not to escalate severely. One determinant of Afghanistan's future will be how it goes about dealing with its past. That brings us to the troubling question of human rights protections.

Human rights and transitional justice

Although the human security paradigm discussed in chapter three implicitly places considerable weight on the protection of human rights, it begs the question of just what "human rights" might entail. While discussion of human rights has historically been rich and subtle,[2] the most useful approaches for a country like Afghanistan bypass complex moral argument about the nature of "rights" and instead focus on positive rights embodied in Articles 22 to 59 of the 2004 constitution, as well as in international humanitarian law instruments such as the 1949 Geneva Convention Relative to the Protection of Civilian Persons in Time of War,[3] and in a range of key multilateral treaties such as the 1948 Convention on the Prevention and Punishment of the Crime of Genocide, the 1966 International Convention on the Elimination of All Forms of Racial Discrimination, the International Covenant on Civil and Political Rights of 1966, the International Covenant on Economic, Social, and Cultural Rights of 1966, the 1979 Convention on the Elimination of All Forms of Discrimination Against Women, and the 1989 Convention on the Rights of the Child. As was noted earlier, the Bonn agreement provided for the establishment of an "independent Human Rights Commission," and while the tasks of national commissions of this kind are almost always difficult to discharge, the Afghan body has proved both creative and courageous, in the face of considerable potential risk to its staff. But that said, the issue of human rights in post-Taliban Afghanistan has been highly controversial, and the controversy has surrounded the explosive subject of transitional justice.

The reason for this is the vast amount of innocent blood that was shed in Afghanistan between 1978 and 2001.[4] That Afghanistan was stained by hideous atrocities during this period is indisputable. The communist era was marked by gross human rights violations,[5] as was the period between the fall of the communist regime and the emergence of the Taliban.[6] These ranged from war crimes to torture and high-level repression of perceived "enemies" and their supporters. The Taliban period, too, witnessed ghastly episodes of mass murder, of which the August 1998 massacres in Mazar-e Sharif were perhaps the worst.[7] The burden of this past weighs heavily on many Afghans, for whom the delivery of justice is a central task of government. Yet the Karzai government has not been at all eager to take up this mantle, and this has led to stinging criticisms of the government, its US backers, and the United Nations.[8]

The central problem has been a perceived tension between justice and peace, at its simplest deriving from the fear that vigorous pursuit of certain past offenders could drive them into active spoiler mode, putting transition as a whole at risk. This might seem a direct conflict between principles and pragmatism, but in reality it is more complex. It actually sets a deontological ethic against an ethic of consequences. In the abstract, there is much to be said for a robust approach to the delivery of justice. It offers some closure for the victims and their families, and can help consolidate a sense that a new state has a genuine commitment to the rule of law. But there are a number of important qualifications.

First, as Helen Durham has put it, "prosecution is not the only model for dealing with the past by states in transition."[9] Various mechanisms have been tested to reconcile victims' needs for justice with the wider societal need to move forward, of which the South African Truth and Reconciliation Commission headed by Archbishop Desmond Tutu was the most innovative. This approach moves beyond merely punitive concepts of justice to focus on restorative notions that increasingly dominate modern criminology. This is not to say that the South African model can simply be exported to another country such as Afghanistan. Particular contexts define what is politically possible and socially meaningful.

Second, it is important to note that domestic courts may be unequal to the task of delivering justice in a way that will do credit to those who sit in judgement on others. The carefully conducted trial of major Nazi war criminals by the International Military Tribunal at Nuremberg in 1945–46 attracted so much attention that less notice was paid to some other trials going on in Europe at the time.[10] Yet in their own ways, these trials were equally instructive, and perhaps the most disturbing was that of the former French prime minister, Pierre Laval, who had thrown in his lot with the collaborationist regime based in the town of Vichy. The presiding judge and jurors made no pretence of impartiality: one juror said to Laval, "You have already been judged by France."[11] Jon Elster, describing this as "a borderline case between legal and political justice," argued that by "judging him according to procedures uncomfortably similar to those of Vichy, the jurors sacrificed the goal of demarcating themselves from the lawless practices of the predecessor regime for the goal of punishing its leaders."[12] Others were even harsher: Pastor Marc Boegner, a critic of Vichy, described the trial as a "scandal beyond description."[13] Some would say exactly the same of the trial of Asadullah Sarwari in Kabul in 2006. Sarwari had headed the communist secret police after the April 1978 coup, and there is no doubt that he was a profoundly repulsive character,[14] but the 2006 trial fell so far short of acceptable standards of probity that even human rights organisations felt bound to protest.[15] The Sarwari trial also highlighted the distinction between political and legal criteria for culpability. To find someone guilty of a serious offence should require specific evidence, not simply generalised suspicion. To treat such suspicion, even if widely shared, as the equivalent of evidence is extremely dangerous.

What this suggests is that before pursuing criminal trials, it is necessary to put in place the basic foundations of the rule of law. So far the progress has been slow. Courts are under-resourced, judges often poorly trained, and a culture of fearless commitment to legality has been battered by the ferocity of political struggle. Furthermore, Afghanistan has no witness-protection program worthy of the name. Some argue that a failure to deal with atrocities of the past means that a "culture of impunity will continue to undermine development of a culture of rule of law."[16] But as the Laval trial showed, there are heavy costs associated with pursuing criminals through debased and corrupted procedures. This does not mean that prosecutions should be permanently stayed, but rather that much more needs to be done before meaningful trials can be held. In the long run, it would make sense to think creatively about ways of integrating traditional and modern institutions. Indeed, Dr Ali Wardak, Reader in Criminology at the University of Glamorgan, has argued that in Afghanistan it may be possible to give effect to some modern principles of restorative justice by making better use of local institutions of informal justice.[17] This is certainly worth exploring.

Positive tendencies

In many media outlets, and perhaps in the popular consciousness in western countries, Afghanistan has registered as a "success story." And there are indeed a number of important positive tendencies at work. It is not manifestly a disaster area of the kind that Iraq has become since the March 2003 invasion, and in significant tracts of the country, particularly in the north and the west, ordinary people are getting on with their lives with some degree of success. The Karzai government may not be much stronger than the Karmal regime in the years following the Soviet invasion, but it enjoys both greater autonomy and a much higher level of popular support. The Karzai government is not a puppet government in the way that the Karmal regime was.

In the period following the Soviet invasion, resistance developed spontaneously in many parts of Afghanistan. There is virtually no mass, spontaneous opposition to the Karzai government. Many Afghans are discontented by the slow progress towards reconstruction, but the armed opposition – in the form of suicide blasts and detonation of improvised explosive devices directed against Coalition forces and NATO troops – is externally driven from bases in Pakistan. Evidence of popular opinion in Afghanistan is encouraging, although sentiment is also potentially volatile. Afghans are largely exhausted by war, open to the idea of rescue, and generally optimistic. A study published shortly before the 2004 presidential election captured this mood. Some 64 per cent of respondents felt that Afghanistan was moving in the right direction, while only 11 per cent felt it was going in the wrong direction. Among this latter 11 per cent, 40 per cent cited dissatisfaction with the performance of the government; only tiny minorities blamed western influence (8 per cent) or the presence of too many foreigners (6 per cent). In the north-east, Ahmad Shah Massoud's old stamping ground, 66 per cent of respondents held favourable opinions of Jihadi leaders, but elsewhere the appraisal of Jihadi leaders was unfavourable.[18] While this survey was conducted in an almost euphoric atmosphere as elections approached, subsequent opinion research remained broadly positive, and a

124

2005 study suggested that frustration with local and provincial government had not translated into opposition to the central government.[19] This is not as odd as one might think: in poor countries, particularly traumatised ones, ordinary people with limited education may nonetheless have an acute understanding of where power and responsibility lie.

A further positive factor is the existence of a sense of Afghan identity alongside other identifications that Afghans routinely make. This is difficult to document, but virtually all specialists who work on Afghanistan are aware of it. The explanation is most likely that Afghans inhabit a territory whose boundaries are accepted by Afghanistan's neighbours, and that Afghanistan as a territorial state enjoys a high level of juridical sovereignty. No neighbouring country has an agenda to annex any part of Afghanistan, and the Afghans' experiences of discrimination in neighbouring countries mean that few would aspire to become citizens of those countries, although many would prefer to live in them temporarily while the situation in Afghanistan resolves itself. This sense of distinctive "Afghan" identity can assist the rulers of the state in securing legitimacy as long as they are not beholden to hostile foreign forces. The Taliban have sought to deride Karzai's credentials as an "Afghan" leader, but how effective this tactic will be remains to be seen, given that their own leadership is based in Quetta in Pakistan and was long intimately linked with Pakistan's military intelligence service. Another factor to note, most pertinent to any attempt that radicals such as al-Qaeda might make to implant themselves in Afghanistan in the future, is that the attitudes of ordinary Afghans to Arabs are far from positive, and Wahhabism of the Saudi variety in particular is widely rejected. This was quite obvious during the 1980s when, as Louis Dupree puts it, the Saudis "spent megabucks among the refugees and resistance fighters in attempts to gain converts for their ultra-conservative, reformist brand of Islam, but with little success."[20] It was not everyday Afghans who created space for al-Qaeda to operate: it was the Taliban, themselves a pathogenic force that reflected a breakdown of social authority in the dislocated environment of the refugee camp.

Also positive has been the drafting of the new constitution and the holding of elections. The process by which the constitution was drafted was far from fully inclusive, but it was a good deal more inclusive than many such processes have historically been. It went well beyond a mere elite compact or settlement, and the delegates at the Constitutional Loya Jirga in many cases arrived full of ideas about good governance (although many of them left with a more realistic sense of the role of behind-the-scenes dealmaking in Afghan politics). While the constitution is not without its defects, there is much in it that is admirable and a tribute to the maturity of those who were involved in crafting it. The holding of elections was an organisational triumph, and there was something deeply moving about the commitment that voters displayed when they showed up at polling places early on the morning of 9 October 2004, most of them to cast votes for the first time in their lives. As in Cambodia in 1993, the early and substantial turnout was a heavy blow to the spoilers who were threatening to disrupt the voting, and represented a courageous display of determination from the citizenry.

Finally, and perhaps most importantly, the flourishing of a relatively free media and civil society has been a very positive development. At the cutting edge have been electronic media such as Radio Arman and Tolo Television, which have attracted large audiences because of their serious yet engaging approaches to important public issues, and their broadcasting of entertainment programs that relieve some of the tedium of people's daily lives. Here they were fortunate to enjoy the protection of an open-minded information and culture minister, Sayed Makhdoom Raheen. Another significant development has been the emergence of a new stratum of young journalists, committed to their craft and competent in their reporting and analysis. These new media actors have on occasion attracted the ire of politicians, and of conservatives in the Supreme Court, but thus far have maintained their positions in the public sphere, albeit somewhat tenuously in the face of death threats and other forms of intimidation. When new institutions are in their infancy, critical media outlets are a vital accountability mechanism, shining spotlights into dark places leaders might prefer to keep hidden. Fostering the development of free media is a task of great importance.

Negative tendencies

Unfortunately, alongside these positive factors are a number of negative ones as well, and they have the potential to outweigh the positive. The tragedy for the bulk of ordinary Afghans is that these negative tendencies are for the most part beyond their direct control. They are either the baggage inevitably associated with decades of disruption, or the product of strategic and tactical calculations at the level of the Afghan political elite or in centres of power beyond Afghanistan's borders. Afghans could be forgiven if they simply lapsed into despair in the face of these challenges; one of the most bracing features of the situation is how many of them are determined to do their best to make their transition process work, even in the face of daunting odds.

The most disturbing negative tendency is that of insecurity. Generating insecurity is the classic tool of the spoiler, and it is a very effective one. Afghanistan so far has been fortunate in one key respect: Kabul has proved largely immune to the kind of terror strikes that have hit some cities and towns in the south, and such attacks as have occurred have been minor when compared to the blitz launched by the Hezb-e Islami between 1992 and 1995, well within the memories of many Kabulis. But even with the presence of the International Security Assistance Force there is no guarantee that this period of stability will continue. In comparison to Baghdad, however, where there are opponents of the Coalition forces comfortably entrenched in the city, there is little evidence of significant terrorist "sleeper cells" in the Afghan capital; most terrorists must enter the city from the countryside. An escalation in bombings in the capital would have detrimental effects on the political atmosphere, not to mention the harm to those inadvertently caught up in the blasts. Given the symbolic importance of capital cities, rural instability does not have such an immediate effect, but once it goes beyond a certain point it too can have damaging consequences, reviving memories of the troubles the United States and its allies faced in Vietnam.

Insecurity to some degree feeds on another negative tendency, namely disappointed expectations. When the Taliban were overthrown, there was widespread relief and a considerable willingness to work with new authorities. In the northern areas of Afghanistan there has been a degree of quiet progress, but the story in the east and south, as noted at a number of points in this book, has been very different. By the beginning of 2006, the situation in the provinces of Kunar, Ghazni, Paktika, Zabul, Kandahar, Uruzgan, and Helmand could realistically be described as critical, with provincial authorities substantially beleaguered. Ironically, these Pushtun-dominated areas, which for the most part voted solidly for Karzai in 2004, are now the areas where his government is most seriously threatened. The insinuation of Taliban from Pakistan is a crucial factor, but poor governance has given them fertile soil in which to plant their messages. Promoting local "strongmen," on the basis that it was better to incorporate them in the state rather than have them engage in spoiler behaviour, miscarried badly. Such figures were often not as strong as they initially appeared but were able to build up their positions after the removal of the Taliban by using their standing within the state to obtain resources and extract further resources from the weak, often in alliance with drug traffickers.

A further negative tendency relates to the central state. While many determined Afghans have given up solid careers in other countries in order to return and serve their country of birth, some of the sad pathologies of the old Afghan state have resurfaced in ways that were detailed in chapter two. Here, it is enough simply to make the point that the functioning of state instrumentalities tends to be shaped by a mixture of past experience and present incentive patterns. There was an opportunity after 2001 to build a different kind of state from those that Afghans had known in the past, but to a large extent the opportunity was missed – not entirely, as the reform processes in the finance ministry and several others showed, but enough to disappoint the public in a range of vital spheres. The most regrettable areas of weakness relate to human resource management and accountability, and this latter area is a critical one, since power that is not subject to checks and balances runs the risk of being abused in serious ways.[21]

Furthermore, the political elite is far from unified, and this could give rise to serious problems. In subtle ways that were perhaps not fully understood at the time, the process of institutional design in post-Taliban Afghanistan has created fissures where there should be bridges. When ministries were handed out as political prizes in 2001 the scene was set for them to become fiefdoms rather than professional bureaucracies; the choice of a presidential system created one winner and many losers; and the Single Non-Transferable Vote system used to elect the Wolesi Jirga created opportunities for unappealing individuals to enter the legislature, who could have been more effectively screened out if they had had to obtain endorsement from parties that were themselves open to scrutiny through a party-registration process. In forging coherent blocs in this kind of situation the obvious symbols are ethnic, and this exposes Afghanistan to the risk of sharpening conflict if ethnic tensions intensify. Controlling such tensions could prove very difficult, given the incentives that ethnic entrepreneurs would have to persist with their agitations.

Finally, Afghanistan is threatened by the sheer depth of its longstanding problems, and by the reluctance of the wider world to empower Afghans to address them. The former should hardly need repeating, but it is easy to forget that even without the disruptions of nearly three decades, Afghanistan would still be an extremely poor country, with serious issues to be addressed through its political processes. The latter is a more general problem for transitions in troubled states. Disruption of the state normally eliminates or disperses some of a country's best talent, and new state agencies are quite likely to be of mixed quality. The temptation for donors faced with nepotism and corruption is to transfer money to agencies which can be relied on to spend it in ways that auditors will find unproblematic. Yet the practical consequence of this approach is often that the good suffer as well as the bad, and "second civil services" flourish so that when commitments dwindle there is not enough local capacity to fill the gap. The result is that funds can be saved in the short run, but costly problems remain to haunt the long run.

Retaining international attention

In the 1942 Academy Award–winning film *Casablanca*, an instructive exchange occurs between the Nazi officer Major Strasser, played by Conrad Veidt, and the Casablanca police official Captain Renault, played by Claude Rains: "Captain Renault, are you entirely certain which side you're on?" asks Strasser, to which Renault replies, "I have no conviction, if that's what you mean. I blow with the wind, and the prevailing wind happens to be from Vichy." Here there is a deep truth, which those managing transitions ignore at their peril. In almost any country, large numbers of people are driven not by ideology but by a desire to survive or prosper on a day-to-day basis. To varying degrees they are watching all the time to see which way the wind is blowing, and they will adjust their own behaviour, and realign themselves politically, accordingly. This casual insight has been refined by social scientists interested in the phenomena of reputational and informational cascades. The former occur when people follow the crowd in order to protect their reputations or standing within it. The classic literary example is found in Hans Christian Andersen's tale of the Emperor's New Clothes, but reputational cascades can have a darker dimension as well, as seen, for example, in the spread of ethnic exclusivism.[22] The latter occur "when people with little personal information about a particular matter base their own beliefs on the apparent beliefs of others."[23] Thus, if the sense begins to develop among some people that international interest is fading and that the Coalition's commitment to support the Karzai government is on the wane, the government's problems could rapidly multiply as that sense starts to spread.

What all this implies is that momentum in transition is enormously important. It is necessary to convince people, through word and deed, not only that times are changing but that there is no going back, that there is no point in persisting with past destructive strategies and tactics because in the new world that is being created they will no longer be effective. The momentum following the Bonn agreement was powerful, but in early 2002, when the United States opposed the expansion of the International Security Assistance Force, a large amount of momentum was lost, and events such as the Constitutional Loya Jirga and the 2004 and 2005 elections were not up to the task of rebuilding it. The importance of the force's expansion as a symbol of change was fully appreciated by Lakhdar Brahimi, who mounted a compelling case for it to proceed without delay. But the US Department of Defense did not grasp its importance for maintaining momentum and seems to have treated the issue as a narrow one of burden-sharing and resource allocation. To Afghans on the ground, the US attitude signalled a mismatch between Washington's words and Washington's deeds. Furthermore, the signal sent by the blocking of the expansion reached an audience not only in Afghanistan but also in Pakistan, and the consequences have proved disastrous. Whatever adjustments western powers and institutions might make to their policies towards Afghanistan, they should be carried out in such a way as to ensure that no further momentum is lost.

The main factor in the blocking of the expansion of the International Security Assistance Force was the looming push by the Bush administration to overthrow the regime of Saddam Hussein in Iraq. The invasion of Iraq in March 2003 created an additional obstacle to Afghanistan's receiving the continuing attention that it deserved. As is by now well documented, the stabilisation of post-invasion Iraq has proved to be a far more complex and difficult task than the administration foresaw, and a much more substantial drain on US financial and military resources.[24] This has affected Afghanistan in two distinct ways. First, the burden of Iraq has pre-occupied decision-makers in key democracies such as the United States and the United Kingdom. This is not to say that Afghanistan has been forgotten, but rather that it has received less sustained attention than should have been the case. Second, faced with domestic difficulties over Iraq, President Bush and his national security team have been driven to paint a rosier picture of Afghanistan than the situation on the ground justifies. The president has presented specific democratic events, such as the 2004 and 2005 elections, as if they amounted to the consolidation of a functioning liberal democracy. Yet the mere holding of elections does not guarantee a democratic political culture, or a consensually unified elite, or an institutionalised political order.[25] As a result, the depth of Afghanistan's problems, and the need for a sustained and long-term approach if they are to be overcome, has not been sufficiently emphasised.

One reason why Afghanistan should have received sustained attention is that it remains a frontline territory for meaningful counterterrorism operations directed against groups associated with Osama Bin Laden, who years after the September 11 attacks remained at large. Yet within a day of the attacks, some key figures in the Bush administration were pushing to shift the focus of a response from Afghanistan to Iraq. This reflected more their long-term preoccupations than any realistic analysis.[26] As Richard A. Clarke, the US national coordinator for security, infrastructure protection and counterterrorism at the time of the attacks, rightly remarked to Secretary of State Colin Powell, "Having been attacked by al Qaeda, for us now to go bombing Iraq in response would be like our invading Mexico after the Japanese attacked us at Pearl Harbor."[27] This in effect was what the US administration did in March 2003, well before the situation in Afghanistan had settled down. Much of Afghanistan could still be used by a group such as al-Qaeda, and were Afghanistan's transition to veer further off course, this could begin to happen again. Finally, it is worth noting that while the attention of western powers might drift away from Afghanistan, the attention of its neighbours would not, and the scope for Pakistani radicals to use Afghan territory for their own purposes would expand.

By way of a conclusion: the need for vigilance

For all the reasons just cited, we might well think that there is no real risk of Afghanistan's being left to fend for itself. The self-interest of states in the wider world should more or less guarantee an ongoing commitment. This is probably true, but the question remains whether the commitment is sufficient in its scale, character, and symbolic significance to put paid to the danger that Afghanistan might drift towards something like the situation in the critical provinces of Iraq. In the crucial period ahead, when the Bonn process has reached its terminus and the path of political transition is increasingly to be mapped by the Afghans themselves, considerable vigilance will be required to keep the country on track. The spoiler problems are considerable, and there is little to suggest that they will soon abate. Much more time is needed to bed down the positive changes that have occurred in recent years, perhaps beyond the patience of western governments seeking to cope with a range of demands on their own time and resources. Furthermore, many of Afghanistan's problems are long-term and developmental, shared with a range of other troubled states, and not amenable to swift solution.

The first phase of the Afghanistan rescue mission came to its conclusion with the elections in September 2005, which marked the end of the road mapped out in Bonn in 2001. Those who have witnessed the highs and lows of this period are unlikely to forget either. The people of Afghanistan have been deeply scarred by the experiences that preceded the Bonn process, and have looked to the transition to address their most acute difficulties. The scorecard at the end of the Bonn phase is inevitably mixed. Some goals that initially seemed improbable have been achieved, but others have remained elusive. The rescue mission has also involved a kaleidoscopic array of actors, with diverse interests, commitments, and capacities. Most have been seeking to do good in their own ways, often in circumstances marked by considerable uncertainties and an absence of established mechanisms to coordinate the efforts of different participants. Alongside those motivated by ambition and self-interest have been others who have contributed vastly more than one might conceivably have expected.

Above all, it has been a very human mission, marked by human frailties but also by great heights of achievement. The philosopher

Kant commented that out of the crooked timber of humanity, no straight thing was ever made.[28] This reflection on the human condition may seem gloomy, but it also suggests that when good results are obtained, we should be willing to praise the efforts of those who have produced them. In that sense, the good that has come from the mission of rescuing Afghanistan is something to celebrate, although it is anything but certain how the mission will finally end.

Epilogue

On 19 December 2005, the new Wolesi Jirga met for the first time in Kabul. While a suicide bombing in the vicinity of the parliament building on 16 December had highlighted the ongoing tensions besetting the Afghan polity, the opening of the parliament seemed an encouraging dawn for a new era. In one of its first moves, the Wolesi Jirga elected Younos Qanuni as its Speaker, and Qanuni in turn relinquished any claim to lead the opposition, signalling an intent to make the new parliament a constructive actor in policy-making rather than simply a venue for destructive grandstanding. In a marker of the oddity of Afghan elite politics, Qanuni won the speakership by defeating Abdul Rab al-Rasoul Sayyaf, whom some of President Karzai's circle of intimates had been promoting.[1] But this did not signify that the Wolesi Jirga was firmly under the control of Karzai's opponents, and on 20 April 2006, he secured its support for the replacement of the respected foreign minister Dr Abdullah with Dr Rangin Dadfar Spanta, a long-term émigré who had been an academic in Germany[2] but lacked either diplomatic experience or proficiency in English, the main language of modern diplomacy. In the process, Karzai rid himself and his government of the last close associate of Ahmad Shah Massoud, the commander who more than any other Afghan had resisted the expansion of Taliban control between 1996 and 2001.[3] He also left the unsettling impression that he was not comfortable with ministers such as Dr Ashraf Ghani and Dr Abdullah, who enjoyed strong international reputations of their own. The Wolesi Jirga's own voting on Karzai's nominees pointed to increasing ethnic polarisation: of the five who were rejected, four were Tajiks and one a Hazara; all Pushtun nominees were approved. Karzai's one female nominee was rejected,[4] as was the courageous information and culture minister, Sayed Makhdoom Raheen. Disturbing reports even began to circulate that a significant bloc in the Wolesi Jirga were actually supporters of Gulbuddin Hekmatyar.[5] Despite his own inclinations, Karzai runs the risk of being dragged more and more in conservative and ethnically chauvinist directions.

From 31 January to 1 February 2006, a major conference on Afghanistan took place in London, co-chaired by Afghanistan and the United Kingdom, and with UN Secretary-General Kofi Annan and US Secretary of State Condoleezza Rice in attendance. In a show of solidarity, Qanuni took part as a prominent member of the Afghan delegation. The conference endorsed a major new Afghanistan Compact, carefully devised in advance of the conference by key donors and the government of Afghanistan, which set out benchmarks and timelines under the headings of "Security," "Governance, Rule of Law and Human Rights," "Economic and Social Development," "Education," "Health," "Agriculture and Rural Development', "Social Protection," and "Economic Governance and Private Sector Development."[6] Secretary Rice delivered a speech full of optimism about Afghanistan's future, and pledged an additional US$1.1 billion for rebuilding the country.

But between the heady rhetoric of solidarity and the hard reality of funding, there was a substantial gulf. In early 2006, the Afghan government had published a new *Afghanistan National Development Strategy*, building on the detailed analysis in *Securing Afghanistan's Future*, which had been prepared for the 2004 Berlin meeting. The conclusions of the *Summary Report* of the strategy were stark. Over five years, Afghanistan would require US$18.865 billion to cover development needs; but domestic revenue was anticipated to amount to US$4.489 billion, not enough even to cover non-development recurrent costs of US$5.453 billion. Therefore US$19.829 billion, or just under US$4 billion per year over five years, would be required in the form of assistance from the wider world.[7] Nothing like this was pledged in London. Donors committed a mere US$10.5 billion for the period from March 2006, barely half the figure Afghanistan needs.[8] As Human Rights Watch pointed out, "reconstruction budgets in Kosovo, Bosnia and East Timor were up to 50 times greater on a per capita basis."[9] A funding shortfall of this magnitude, while perhaps explicable in terms of limited absorptive capacity, not only runs the risk of compromising the momentum of a political transition, but also sends the worst kind of signal to those who would wish to see Afghanistan's transition fail, virtually inviting them to redouble their spoiling endeavours.[10]

And all the indications are that spoilers are a problem of mounting seriousness. In early May 2006, the highly experienced *New York Times* correspondent Carlotta Gall filed a report from the southern province of Uruzgan that should serve as a wake-up call to anyone regarding the Afghan situation with complacency. The Taliban, she wrote, "appear to be moving their insurgency into a new phase, flooding the rural areas of southern Afghanistan with weapons and men." She went on to note that "the scale of the militants' presence and their sheer brazenness have alarmed Afghans and foreign officials far more than in previous years," and that the "arrival of large numbers of Taliban in the villages, flush with money and weapons, has dealt a blow to public confidence in the Afghan government, already undermined by lack of tangible progress and frustration with corrupt and ineffective leaders." The most chilling observation came from a shopkeeper in Tirik Kot named Haji Safiullah: "During the day the people, the police and the army are with the government, but during the night, the people, the police and the army are all with the Taliban and Al Qaeda."[11] It is into this maelstrom that Australian troops are shortly to deploy as part of a new Provincial Reconstruction Team, but the task they face is plainly awesome.[12] The price of the early loss of momentum in the Afghan transition is proving to be much higher than was expected.

Even Kabul is less of an island of stability than on occasion it might have appeared. At 8 am on 29 May 2006, a truck in a US military convoy entering Kabul from the north via the Khair Khana pass crashed into a row of vehicles trapped in rush-hour traffic, killing a number of commuters. This triggered an outburst of fury on the part of Afghans long angered by the aggressive driving tactics of the Coalition, and within a short time rioting had spread to other parts of the city. The CARE International office in Shahr-e Naw was set ablaze, NATO forces were obliged to evacuate officials from the European Union office across the road, and shops, offices, and the new Serena Hotel were damaged as gunfire echoed through downtown Kabul. For the first time in four years, the government was forced to impose a night-time curfew. Prompt deployment of the Afghan National Army choked off further protests, and Karzai condemned the rioters as "enemies of Afghanistan."[13] Yet the frustrations underlying outbursts of this kind are real, and if they are not addressed soon, more trouble will surely follow.

Thus, Afghanistan remains on a knife-edge, confronted by brutal insurgents at home and diminishing interest abroad.[14] The patience of at least some Afghans is beginning to wear perilously thin, and the best response to this challenge is not more "quick impact" projects, but better rule. It is not too late to save the situation, but the rescue mission that was triggered on 11 September 2001 has not been completed. The key challenge for the president of Afghanistan is to use his significant formal powers to shape a government that is competent, effective, inclusive, and clean. The key challenge for those of us in the wider world is to match our rhetoric with commitments. If we manage to do so, the Afghan people will have reasonable prospects of a reasonably decent future. If we fail to do so, it will tell us very little about the Afghans, but a great deal about ourselves.

Acknowledgements

On the way to writing this book, I have accumulated a number of debts. Many are to people who would prefer not to be specifically named, and I would like to thank them for the candour of the views they shared with me.

Happily, there are others whom I can acknowledge more explicitly. Various ideas in this book were initially aired in lectures or seminars at the Afghanistan Research and Evaluation Unit in Kabul; at the Woodrow Wilson International Center for Scholars, the Middle East Institute, and the Bureau of Intelligence and Research at the US Department of State in Washington DC; at the Jamia Millia Islamia University in New Delhi; at symposia in Tokyo organised by the Japan Centre for Area Studies; at conferences in Princeton, Vienna, and Istanbul organised by the Liechtenstein Institute for Self-Determination at Princeton University; and at Monash University, the University of Western Australia, and the Australian National University. I would like to thank the organisers of these gatherings for their hospitality, and the participants for their stimulating comments. In addition to these institutions, I have benefited greatly from conversations or longer discussions with Reginald Austin, David Avery, Lakhdar Brahimi, Wolfgang Danspeckgruber, Pierre Centlivres, Micheline Centlivres-Demont, Mohammad Eshaq, Robert P. Finn, Ashraf Ghani, Frédéric Grare, Dumisani Hanyani, Chris Johnson, Bruce Koepke, Jolyon Leslie, Saad Mohseni, Yassin Mohseni, Ahmed Rashid, Haider Reza, Barnett R. Rubin, Susanne Schmeidl, Scott Smith, Barbara Stapleton, Astri Suhrke, J. Alexander Thier, Julian Type, Francesc Vendrell, Ali Wardak, Farouq Wardak, Marvin G. Weinbaum, and Samina Yasmeen. I would particularly like to thank Peter Browne of the Institute for Social Research, Swinburne

University of Technology, for his very helpful comments on the entire manuscript of this book.

As ever, I owe a very great debt to Amin Saikal and Fazel Haq Saikal, with whom I have been discussing Afghan politics on an almost daily basis for many years. Just after the collapse of the communist regime in Kabul, Fazel Saikal and I included a chapter on "Free and Fair Elections" in a monograph we wrote for the International Peace Academy entitled *Political Order in Post-Communist Afghanistan* (Boulder: Lynne Rienner, 1992). Our suggestions seemed to have fallen dead from the press, but a number came to life after 2001! He and I were able to observe the 2004 and 2005 elections in Afghanistan as guests of the Joint Electoral Management Body, and I would like to thank the JEMB and its staff for their generous support, and Fazel for being a delightfully irreverent partner in the observation process.

A special word of thanks is due to my mother, Jean Maley, who has thus far not accepted my suggestion that she join me on a visit to Afghanistan, and now at the age of 85 may have closed her mind to the possibility. Nonetheless, I live in hope, and thank her for her patience as I have pursued what must often strike her as a very obscure interest.

Finally, I would like to thank Pauline Kerr, Andrea Haese, and Kaye Eldridge, my colleagues at the Asia-Pacific College of Diplomacy, for providing such a congenial and tolerant milieu for a peripatetic director.

William Maley
Asia-Pacific College of Diplomacy
Australian National University

References

Introduction

1. For discussions of the evolution of the Afghan state, see Christine Noelle, *State and Tribe in Nineteenth-Century Afghanistan: The Reign of Amir Dost Muhammad Khan* (1826–1863) (Richmond: Curzon Press, 1998); Vartan Gregorian, *The Emergence of Modern Afghanistan: Politics of Reform and Modernization 1880–1946* (Stanford: Stanford University Press, 1969); Hasan Kawun Kakar, *Government and Society in Afghanistan; The Reign of Amir 'Abd al-Rahman Khan* (Austin: University of Texas Press, 1979); Leon B. Poullada, *Reform and Rebellion in Afghanistan: King Amanullah's Failure to Modernize a Tribal Society* (Ithaca: Cornell University Press, 1973); and Amin Saikal, *Modern Afghanistan: A History of Struggle and Survival* (London: I. B. Tauris, 2004).

2. For details, see Henry S. Bradsher, *Afghan Communism and Soviet Intervention* (Karachi: Oxford University Press, 1999); Barnett R. Rubin, *The Fragmentation of Afghanistan: State Formation and Collapse in the International System* (New Haven: Yale University Press, 2002); and William Maley, *The Afghanistan Wars* (New York: Palgrave Macmillan, 2002).

3. On the Soviet intervention, see Anthony Arnold, *Afghanistan: The Soviet Invasion in Perspective* (Stanford: Hoover Institution Press, 1985); Henry S. Bradsher, *Afghanistan and the Soviet Union* (Durham: Duke University Press, 1985); Douglas A. Borer, *Superpowers Defeated: Vietnam and Afghanistan Compared* (London: Frank Cass, 1999); and Odd Arne Westad, *The Global Cold War* (Cambridge: Cambridge University Press, 2005), pp 299–330. On the final withdrawal, see Amin Saikal and William Maley (eds), *The Soviet Withdrawal from Afghanistan* (Cambridge: Cambridge University Press, 1989).

4. On Islamic influences on the Afghan resistance, see Olivier Roy, *Islam and Resistance in Afghanistan* (Cambridge: Cambridge University Press, 1990); Asta Olesen, *Islam and Politics in Afghanistan* (Richmond: Curzon Press, 1995); and David B. Edwards, *Before Taliban: Genealogies of the Afghan Jihad* (Berkeley & Los Angeles: University of California Press, 2002), Part III.

5. On the pragmatic dimensions of Afghan Islam, see Thomas Barfield, "An Islamic State is a State Run by Good Muslims: Religion as a Way of Life and Not an Ideology in Afghanistan," in Robert W. Hefner (ed.), *Remaking Muslim Politics: Pluralism, Contestation, Democratization* (Princeton: Princeton University Press, 2005), pp 213–39.

6. See Maley, *The Afghanistan Wars*, pp 8, 71, 154.

7. Gavin Bell, "Paradise Lost in Afghan Valley of Death," *The Times*, 21 July 1987.

8. On the background of the Taliban see William Maley (ed.), *Fundamentalism Reborn?: Afghanistan and the Taliban* (London: Hurst & Co., 1998); Ahmed Rashid, *Taliban: Militant Islam, Oil and Fundamentalism in Central Asia* (New Haven: Yale University Press, 2000); Gilles Dorronsoro, *Revolution Unending: Afghanistan, 1979 to the Present* (New York: Columbia University Press, 2005), pp 233–311; and Maley, *The Afghanistan Wars*, pp 218–250.

9. Barnett R. Rubin, "Constructing Sovereignty for Security," *Survival*, vol 47, no 4, Winter 2005, pp 93–106 at p 98.

10. For detailed discussion of the nature of humanitarian intervention, see Nicholas J. Wheeler, *Saving Strangers: Humanitarian Intervention in International Society* (Oxford: Oxford University Press, 2000); and Simon Chesterman, *Just War or Just Peace? Humanitarian Intervention and International Law* (Oxford: Oxford University Press, 2001).

11. See Simon Chesterman, "Humanitarian Intervention and Afghanistan," in Jennifer M. Welsh (ed.), *Humanitarian Intervention and International Relations* (Oxford: Oxford University Press, 2004), pp 163–175 at p 163.

12. See William Maley, *The Foreign Policy of the Taliban* (New York: Council on Foreign Relations, 2000), pp 12–14.

13. See *The Responsibility to Protect: Report of the International Commission on Intervention and State Sovereignty* (Ottawa: International Development Research Centre, 2001).

14. *Shorter Oxford English Dictionary on Historical Principles* (Oxford: Oxford University Press, 2002), vol II, p 2543.

15. Some might see such patronising approaches as a species of Orientalism, in Edward Said's sense of "a Western style for dominating, restructuring, and having authority over the Orient": see Edward W. Said, *Orientalism* (London: Routledge & Kegan Paul, 1978), p 3. However, rescuers can act in a patronising way to people and peoples from many

different places: General de Gaulle's notoriously tense relations with the Allies during the Second World War stand as testimony to this phenomenon. Vulnerable actors can easily be stereotyped. So, of course, can the powerful: see Ian Buruma and Avishai Margalit, *Occidentalism: The West in the Eyes of Its Enemies* (New York: The Penguin Press, 2004).

16. Maley, *The Afghanistan Wars*, p 283.

1. The nature of Afghanistan's problems

1. See William Maley, "The Reconstruction of Afghanistan," in Ken Booth and Tim Dunne (eds), *Worlds in Collision: Terror and the Future of Global Order* (London: Palgrave Macmillan, 2002), pp 184–93.

2. See William Maley, "Democratic Governance and Post-Conflict Transitions," *Chicago Journal of International Law*, vol 6, no 2, Winter 2006, pp 683–701; and also Thomas Carothers, *Critical Mission: Essays on Democracy Promotion* (Washington DC: Carnegie Endowment for International Peace, 2004), pp 167–83.

3. Robert H. Jackson, *Quasi-States: Sovereignty, International Relations, and the Third World* (Cambridge: Cambridge University Press, 1990).

4. Gianfranco Poggi, *The State: Its Nature, Development and Prospects* (Stanford: Stanford University Press, 1990), p 19.

5. Joel S. Migdal, *State in Society: Studying How States and Societies Transform and Constitute One Another* (Cambridge: Cambridge University Press, 2001), pp 15–16.

6. There is by now an extensive literature on "state failure." For useful surveys, see Nelson Kasfir, "Domestic Anarchy, Security Dilemmas, and Violent Predation: Causes of Failure," in Robert I. Rotberg (ed.), *When States Fail: Causes and Consequences* (Princeton: Princeton University Press, 2004), pp 53–76; Sebastian von Einsiedel, "Policy Responses to State Failure," in Simon Chesterman, Michael Ignatieff and Ramesh Thakur (eds), *Making States Work: State Failure and the Crisis of Governance* (Tokyo: United Nations University Press, 2005), pp 13–35.

7. *Select Works of Edmund Burke* (Indianapolis: Liberty Fund, 1999), vol I, p 236.

8. See Amin Saikal and William Maley, *Regime Change in Afghanistan: Foreign Intervention and the Politics of Legitimacy* (Boulder: Westview, 1991).

9. Joel S. Migdal, *Strong Societies and Weak States: State–Society Relations and State Capabilities in the Third World* (Princeton: Princeton University Press, 1988), p 4.

10. Thomas J. Barfield, "Weak Links on a Rusty Chain: Structural Weaknesses in Afghanistan's Provincial Government Administration," in M. Nazif Shahrani and Robert L. Canfield (eds), *Revolutions and Rebellions in Afghanistan: Anthropological Perspectives* (Berkeley: Institute of International Studies, University of California, 1984), pp 170–84.

11. See Hasan Kakar, "The Fall of the Afghan Monarchy in 1973," *International Journal of Middle East Studies*, vol 9, 1978, pp 195–214 at p 200.

12. Ralph H. Magnus, "The Military and Politics in Afghanistan: Before and After the Revolution," in Edward A. Olsen and Stephen Jurika, Jnr (eds), *The Armed Forces in Contemporary Asian Societies* (Boulder: Westview Press, 1986), pp 325–44 at p 335.

13. Barnett R. Rubin, *The Fragmentation of Afghanistan: State Formation and Collapse in the International System* (New Haven: Yale University Press, 2002), p 296.

14. See Russell Hardin, "Do We Want Trust in Government?," in Mark E. Warren (ed.), *Democracy and Trust* (Cambridge: Cambridge University Press, 1999), pp 22–41.

15. Barbara A. Misztal, *Trust in Modern Societies* (Oxford: Polity Press, 1996), p 24.

16. Charles Tilly, *Trust and Rule* (Cambridge: Cambridge University Press, 2005), p 12.

17. See Bernt Glatzer, "Is Afghanistan on the Brink of Ethnic and Tribal Disintegration?," in William Maley (ed), *Fundamentalism Reborn? Afghanistan and the Taliban* (London: Hurst & Co., 1998), pp 167–81 at pp 177–178.

18. On social complexity in Afghanistan, see Erwin Orywal (ed), *Die ethnischen Gruppen Afghanistans: Fallstudien zu Gruppenidentität und Intergruppenbeziehungen* (Wiesbaden: Dr. Ludwig Reichert Verlag, 1986); Conrad Schetter, *Ethnizität und ethnische Konflikte in Afghanistan* (Berlin: Dietrich Reimer Verlag, 2003).

19. See William Maley, "Social Dynamics and the Disutility of Terror: Afghanistan, 1978–1989," in P. Timothy Bushnell, Vladimir Shlapentokh, Christopher K. Vanderpool, and Jeyaratnam Sundram (eds), *State Organized Terror: The Case of Violent Internal Repression* (Boulder CO: Westview Press, 1991), pp 113–31.

20. See William Maley, "Institutional Design and the Rebuilding of Trust," in William Maley, Charles Sampford and Ramesh Thakur (eds), *From Civil Strife to Civil Society: Civil and Military Responsibilities in Disrupted*

States (Tokyo: United Nations University Press, 2003), pp 163–79 at pp 166–67.

21. See David B. Edwards, "Summoning Muslims: Print, Politics, and Religious Ideology in Afghanistan," *Journal of Asian Studies*, vol 53, no 3, 1993, pp 609–28.

22. Sarah Kenyon Lischer, *Dangerous Sanctuaries: Refugee Camps, Civil War, and the Dilemmas of Humanitarian Aid* (Ithaca: Cornell University Press, 2005), p 52.

23. See Rubin, *The Fragmentation of Afghanistan*, p 249.

24. For an extremely insightful discussion of the diverse functions of refugee camps, see Fiona Terry, *Condemned to Repeat? The Paradox of Humanitarian Action* (Ithaca: Cornell University Press, 2002).

25. On Arab combatants and trainees, see Barnett R. Rubin, "Arab Islamists in Afghanistan," in John L. Esposito (ed.), *Political Islam: Revolution, Radicalism, or Reform?* (Boulder: Lynne Rienner, 1997), pp 179–206. On the impact of Afghanistan on Southeast Asia, see International Crisis Group, *Jemaah Islamiyah in Southeast Asia: Damaged but Still Dangerous* (Brussels: International Crisis Group, Asia Report no 63, 26 August 2003).

26. See William Maley, *The Afghanistan Wars* (New York: Palgrave Macmillan, 2002), pp 226–28.

27. BBC Newshour, 3 October 1996.

28. "The India Imperative: A Conversation with Robert D. Blackwill," *The National Interest*, no 80, Summer 2005, pp 9–17 at p 12.

29. For details, see *Afghanistan: The Massacre in Mazar-i Sharif* (New York: Human Rights Watch, 1998).

30. See John Gray, *Al Qaeda and What it Means to be Modern* (London: Faber & Faber, 2003).

31. See Voter Education Planning Survey, *Afghanistan 2004 National Elections. A Report Based on a Public Opinion Poll* (Washington DC: The Asia Foundation, July 2004), pp 29–30; Rebecca Linder, *Voices of a New Afghanistan* (Washington DC: Post-Conflict Reconstruction Project, Center for Strategic and International Studies, June 2005), p 17.

32. See Lucien W. Pye, *Warlord Politics: Conflict and Coalition in the Modernization of Republican China* (New York: Praeger, 1971); Hsi-Sheng Ch'i, *Warlord Politics in China 1916–1928* (Stanford: Stanford University Press, 1976). For more general discussions, see John Mackinlay, "Defining Warlords," *International Peacekeeping*, vol 7, no 1, Spring 2000, pp 48–62;

Antonio Giustozzi, *Respectable Warlords? The Politics of State-Building in Post-Taleban Afghanistan* (London: Crisis States Programme Working Papers Series no 1, Working Paper no 33, Development Research Centre, London School of Economics and Political Science, September 2003); and Sasha Lezhnev, *Crafting Peace: Strategies to Deal with Warlords in Collapsing States* (Lanham: Lexington Books, 2005), pp 1–12.

33. See Chris Johnson and Jolyon Leslie, *Afghanistan: The Mirage of Peace* (London: Zed Books, 2004), p 162.

34. See Antonio Giustozzi, *"Good" State vs. "Bad" Warlords? A Critique of State-Building Strategies in Afghanistan* (London: Crisis States Programme Working Papers Series no 1, WP no 51, Development Research Centre, London School of Economics and Political Science, October 2004).

35. See Johnson and Leslie, *Afghanistan: The Mirage of Peace*, p 163. Sayyaf is altogether more threatening a figure than Muhammad Qasim Fahim. Sayyaf has strong ideological commitments of a kind that Fahim has never displayed, and furthermore operates through informal influence over conservative jurists; his position as a member of the Wolesi Jirga elected in September 2005 is not at all the source of his significance. On Sayyaf, see William Maley, "The Future of Political Islam in Afghanistan," in Shahram Akbarzadeh and Samina Yasmeen (eds), *Islam and the West: Reflections from Australia* (Sydney: UNSW Press, 2005), pp 77–92 at pp 86–87.

36. On Pakistan's connections with radical Afghan groups, see Rizwan Hussain, *Pakistan and the Emergence of Islamic Militancy in Afghanistan* (Aldershot: Ashgate, 2005).

37. See William Maley, "The Perils of Pipelines," *The World Today*, vol 54, no 8–9, August–September 1998, pp 231–32.

38. For a detailed discussion, see Shahram Akbarzadeh, *Uzbekistan and the United States: Authoritarianism, Islamism and Washington's Security Agenda* (London: Zed Books, 2005).

39. "The India Imperative: A Conversation with Robert D. Blackwill," p 12.

40. Olivier Roy, *The Lessons of the Soviet/Afghan War* (London: Adelphi Paper no 259, International Institute for Strategic Studies, 1991), p 37.

41. For accounts of US engagement with the Afghanistan issue during this period, see *The 9/11 Commission Report: Final Report of the National Commission on Terrorist Attacks Upon the United States* (New York: W. W. Norton, 2004), pp 174–214; and Steve Coll, *Ghost Wars: The Secret History of the CIA, Afghanistan, and Bin Laden, From the Soviet Invasion to September 10, 2001* (London: Penguin Books, 2005).

42. See Minton F. Goldman, "President Bush and Afghanistan: A Turning Point in American Policy," *Comparative Strategy*, vol 11, no 2, 1992, pp 177–93.

43. Kenneth Katzman, *Afghanistan: Post-War Governance, Security, and U.S. Policy* (Washington DC: Congressional Research Service, The Library of Congress, May 19, 2005), p 5.

44. Anthony Davis, "How the Afghan War Was Won," *Jane's Intelligence Review*, vol 14, no 2, 2002, pp 6–13 at p 7.

2. Reconstituting the political system

1. S. Frederick Starr, "Sovereignty and Legitimacy in Afghan Nation-Building," in Francis Fukuyama (ed.), *Nation-Building: Beyond Afghanistan and Iraq* (Baltimore: The Johns Hopkins University Press, 2006), pp 107–24 at pp 109, 112, 118–22, 124.

2. See Carlotta Gall, "Taliban Rebels Still Menacing Afghan South," *New York Times*, 2 March 2006; Sébastien Trives, "Afghanistan: Réduire l'Insurrection. Le Cas du Sud-est," *Politique étrangère*, no 1, 2006, pp 105–18.

3. For more detailed discussion of the Bonn process, see J. Alexander Thier, "The Politics of Peace-Building. Year One: From Bonn to Kabul," in Antonio Donini, Norah Niland and Karin Wermester (eds), *Nation-Building Unraveled? Aid, Peace and Justice in Afghanistan* (Bloomfield: Kumarian Press, 2004), pp 39–60; William Maley, "State-Building and Political Development in Afghanistan," in Masako Ishii and Jacqueline A. Siapno (eds), *Between Knowledge and Commitment: Post-Conflict Peacebuilding and Reconstruction in Regional Contexts* (Osaka: JCAS Symposium Series no 21, Japan Center for Area Studies, National Museum of Ethnology, 2004), pp 165–83.

4. Karzai was forthright in publicly pressing the United States to take a stronger line against the Taliban, notably at a Capitol Hill Policymakers Forum organised by the Afghanistan Foundation at which he and I spoke in Washington DC on 28 September 1999.

5. A trivial example: in mid-September 2003, I attended a function in Kabul at which Karzai spoke. His arrival was preceded by a search of the venue by American guards with a large and ferocious-looking sniffer-dog. The disapproval of the Afghan guests at this intrusion was very obvious. From late 2005, the protection of the president became the responsibility of a new Afghan presidential protective service.

6. See Amy Waldman, "In Afghanistan, U.S. Envoy Sits in Seat of Power,"

New York Times, 17 April 2004; Jon Lee Anderson, "The Man in the Palace: Hamid Karzai and the Dilemma of Being Afghanistan's President," *New Yorker*, 6 June 2005, pp 60–73.

7. See Marina Ottaway and Anatol Lieven, *Rebuilding Afghanistan: Fantasy versus Reality* (Washington DC: Policy Brief no 12, Carnegie Endowment for International Peace, 2002).

8. Chris Johnson and Jolyon Leslie, *Afghanistan: The Mirage of Peace* (London: Zed Books, 2004), p 157.

9. On such aspirations, see Gilles Dorronsoro, *Revolution Unending: Afghanistan, 1979 to the Present* (New York: Columbia University Press, 2005), pp 322–24; Gary C. Schroen, *First In: An Insider's Account of How the CIA Spearheaded the War on Terror in Afghanistan* (New York: Ballantine Books, 2005), pp 98, 146, 162–64.

10. Keith B. Richburg, "Karzai Replaces Top Deputy on Ticket," *Washington Post*, 27 July 2004.

11. The importance of effective state-building was emphasised in a range of specialist commentaries. See Astri Suhrke, Arne Strand, and Kristian Berg Harpviken, *Peace-Building Strategies for Afghanistan. Part I: Lessons from Past Experiences in Afghanistan* (Bergen: Chr. Michelson Institute, 2002); Astri Suhrke, Arne Strand, and Kristian Berg Harpviken, *Peace-Building Strategies for Afghanistan. Part II: A Decade of Peace-Building: Lessons for Afghanistan* (Bergen: Chr. Michelson Institute, 2002); Andreas Wimmer and Conrad Schetter, *State-Formation First: Recommendations for Reconstruction and Peacemaking in Afghanistan* (Bonn: Discussion Papers on Development Policy no 45, Center for Development Research, 2002); and Chris Johnson, William Maley, Alexander Thier and Ali Wardak, *Afghanistan's Political and Constitutional Development* (London: Overseas Development Institute, 2003).

12. Joel S. Migdal, "The State in Society: An Approach to Struggles for Domination," in Joel S. Migdal, Atul Kohli and Vivienne Shue (eds), *State Power and Social Forces: Domination and Transformation in the Third World* (Cambridge: Cambridge University Press, 1994), pp 7–34 at p 16.

13. Anne Evans, Nick Manning, Yasin Osmani, Anne Tully and Andrew Wilder, *A Guide to Government in Afghanistan* (Kabul: Afghanistan Research and Evaluation Unit, 2004) pp 12–21.

14. On "scope" and "strength" as key parameters of state-building, see Francis Fukuyama, *State-Building: Governance and World Order in the 21st Century* (Ithaca: Cornell University Press, 2004), pp 6–14.

15. *Afghanistan: State Building, Sustaining Growth, and Reducing Poverty* (Washington DC: The World Bank, 2005), pp 46–47.

16. See Anne Evans, Nick Manning, and Anne Tully with Yasin Osmani and Andrew Wilder, *Subnational Administration in Afghanistan: Assessment and Recommendations for Action* (Kabul: Afghanistan Research and Evaluation Unit, 2004); and Anne Evans and Yasin Osmani, *Assessing Progress: Update Report on Subnational Administration in Afghanistan* (Kabul: Afghanistan Research and Evaluation Unit, 2005).

17. See Mark E. Warren, *Democracy and Association* (Princeton: Princeton University Press, 2001).

18. See Mancur Olson, *The Logic of Collective Action: Public Goods and the Theory of Groups* (Cambridge: Harvard University Press, 1965).

19. See Frank Reber and Susanne Schmeidl, "Die Stimmen der Afghanischen Zivilgesellschaft: Das Afghan Civil Society Meeting als Hoffnungsträger," *Afghanistan Info*, no 50, March 2002, pp 15–16.

20. *Afghanistan: National Human Development Report 2004. Security with a Human Face: Challenges and Responsibilities* (Kabul: United Nations Development Programme, 2004), pp 137–41.

21. Nicholas Leader and Mohammed Haneef Atmar, "Political Projects: Reform, Aid and the State in Afghanistan," in Antonio Donini, Norah Niland and Karin Wermester (eds), *Nation-Building Unraveled? Aid, Peace and Justice in Afghanistan* (Bloomfield: Kumarian Press, 2004), pp 166–86 at p 172. (Atmar served as Afghanistan's rural reconstruction and development minister from June 2002.)

22. See Inger W. Boesen, *From Subjects to Citizens: Local Participation in the National Solidarity Programme* (Kabul: Afghanistan Research and Evaluation Unit, 2004); Alessandro Monsutti, "La Fauss e Monnaie ou la Candeur Coupable," *Afghanistan Info*, no 55, October 2004, pp 10–12.

23. Johnson and Leslie, *Afghanistan: The Mirage of Peace*, p 190.

24. See Graham Maddox, "Constitution," in Terence Ball, James Farr, and Russell L. Hanson (eds), *Political Innovation and Conceptual Change* (Cambridge: Cambridge University Press, 1989), pp 50–67.

25. See Andrew MacIntyre, *The Power of Institutions: Political Architecture and Governance* (Ithaca: Cornell University Press, 2003).

26. On the design process, see Barnett R. Rubin, "Crafting a Constitution for Afghanistan," *Journal of Democracy*, vol 15, no 3, July 2004, pp 5–19. The briefing papers prepared for the Commission can be found in

Afghanistan: Towards a New Constitution (New York: Center on International Cooperation, New York University, 2003).

27. Amy Waldman and Carlotta Gall, "A Young Afghan Dares to Mention the Unmentionable," *New York Times*, 18 December 2003.

28. For the Dari text and an English translation of the constitution, see Nadjma Yassari (ed.), *The Shari'a in the Constitutions of Afghanistan, Iran and Egypt: Implications for Private Law* (Tübingen: Mohr Siebeck, 2005), pp 269–329. My references to articles of the constitution largely follow this translation, but on occasion depart from it for the sake of greater precision. (Since, under Article 16 of the 2004 constitution, Dari and Pushto are the official languages of Afghanistan, no single English translation of the constitution is authoritative and official.)

29. For more detailed discussion of this provision, see Mohammad Hashim Kamali, "Islam and its Shari'a in the Afghan Constitution 2004 with Special Reference to Personal Law," in Nadjma Yassari (ed.), *The Shari'a in the Constitutions of Afghanistan, Iran and Egypt: Implications for Private Law* (Tübingen: Mohr Siebeck, 2005), pp 23–43 at pp 36–38.

30. See J. Alexander Thier, "Attacking Democracy from the Bench," *New York Times*, 26 January 2004.

31. See Carlotta Gall, "Afghan Talks Adjourn, Deeply Divided on Ethnic Lines," *New York Times*, 2 January 2004.

32. See Matthew Soberg Shugart and John M. Carey, *Presidents and Assemblies: Constitutional Design and Electoral Dynamics* (Cambridge: Cambridge University Press, 1992).

33. Juan Linz, "The Perils of Presidentialism," *Journal of Democracy*, vol 1, no 1, 1990, pp 51–69.

34. Jørgen Elklit and Palle Svensson, "What Makes Elections Free and Fair?," *Journal of Democracy*, vol 8, no 3, 1997, pp 32–46 at p 35.

35. *The Political Transition in Iraq: Report of the Fact-Finding Mission* (New York: United Nations, S/2004/140, 23 February 2004), para 40.

36. To prevent multiple voting, the Procedures Manual distributed to the 125,000-odd polling staff provided that indelible ink should be applied to the cuticle of a voter's left thumb as an indicator that the person should not be permitted to vote again. The manual contained a drawing showing a pen-like applicator being used to apply the ink. However, in some kits of voting materials, the indelible ink was supplied in a white plastic container, and most kits contained a standard whiteboard marker (to be used for other purposes) which contained non-indelible ink. At some polling

places, confused staff mistakenly used the latter to mark voters' thumbs. The consequence was that some voters found that they could wipe off the ink that had been applied to their thumbnails. However, an expert report concluded that "multiple voting was not a significant problem on Election Day": see *Final Report of Impartial Panel of Election Experts Concerning Afghanistan Presidential Election 2004* (Kabul: Impartial Panel of Election Experts, 1 November 2004), p 21.

37. For this reason, the SNTV system is poorly regarded among specialists on electoral systems: see Shaun Bowler, David M. Farrell and Robin T. Pettitt, "Expert Opinion on Electoral Systems: So Which Electoral System is 'Best'?," *Journal of Elections, Public Opinion and Parties*, vol 15, no 1, April 2005, pp 3–19.

38. See Gerald M. Pomper, "Concepts of Political Parties," *Journal of Theoretical Politics*, vol 4, no 2, April 1992, pp 143–59.

39. For the most detailed discussion of this earlier experience of parliamentarism, see Marvin G. Weinbaum, "The Legislator as Intermediary: Integration of the Center and Periphery in Afghanistan," in Albert F. Eldridge (ed.), *Legislatures in Plural Societies: The Search for Cohesion in National Development* (Durham: Duke University Press, 1977) pp 95–121.

40. Andrew Wilder, *A House Divided? Analysing the 2005 Afghan Elections* (Kabul: Afghanistan Research and Evaluation Unit, 2005), pp 5, 7, 8, 14.

41. Ibid, p 32.

42. See M. J. C. Vile, *Constitutionalism and the Separation of Powers* (London: Oxford University Press, 1967).

43. See Stéphane Guimbert and Joachim Wehner, "Making the New Fiscal Constitution Work," in Michael Carnahan et al (eds), *Reforming Fiscal and Economic Management in Afghanistan* (Washington DC: The World Bank, 2004), pp 81–93.

44. See M. Steven Fish, "Stronger Legislatures, Stronger Democracies," *Journal of Democracy*, vol 17, no 1, January 2006, pp 5–20.

45. The remainder of this paragraph draws on William Maley, "Making a Presidential System Work," *Afghanistan Info*, no 56, March 2005, pp 10–11, which in turn is based on a lecture delivered at the Afghanistan Research and Evaluation Unit in Kabul on 12 October 2004.

46. See Eugene Kamenka, *Bureaucracy* (Oxford: Basil Blackwell, 1989).

47. Max Weber, "Bureaucracy," in H. H. Gerth and C. Wright Mills (eds), *From Max Weber: Essays in Sociology* (London: Routledge & Kegan Paul, 1948), pp 196–244 at pp 196–98.

48. *Afghanistan: State Building, Sustaining Growth, and Reducing Poverty*, p 52.

49. *Afghanistan: Managing Public Finances for Development* (Washington DC: The World Bank, Report no 34582–AF, 22 December 2005), vol I, p 21.

50. *Afghanistan: State Building, Sustaining Growth, and Reducing Poverty*, p 47.

51. *Afghanistan: Managing Public Finances for Development*, vol I, p 15.

52. On legitimacy, see Ashraf Ghani, Clare Lockhart and Michael Carnahan, *Closing the Sovereignty Gap: An Approach to State-Building* (London: Working Paper no 253, Overseas Development Institute, September 2005), p 11. On transparency, see Ashraf Ghani, Clare Lockhart and Michael Carnahan, "An Agenda for State-Building in the Twenty-First Century," *Fletcher Forum of World Affairs*, vol 30, no 1, Winter 2006, pp 101–23 at p 20.

3. Rebuilding security

1. Carlotta Gall, "Afghan Officials Blame Taliban in the Killing of 12 Civilians," *New York Times*, 9 January 2004.

2. See, for example, George Packer, *The Assassins' Gate: America in Iraq* (New York: Farrar, Straus and Giroux, 2005).

3. See Kimberly Zisk Marten, *Enforcing the Peace: Learning from the Imperial Past* (New York: Columbia University Press, 2004).

4. See John J. Mearsheimer, *The Tragedy of Great Power Politics* (New York, NY: W. W. Norton, 2001).

5. For more detailed discussion of human security, see William Maley, "A 'War Against Terrorism'? Afghanistan, Iraq and Palestine," in Chika Obiya and Hidemitsu Kuroki (eds), *Political Violence and Human Security in the Post 9.11 World* (Osaka: JCAS Symposium Series no 24, Japan Center for Area Studies, 2006), pp 149–64 at pp 150–53.

6. See Jessica Tuchman Mathews, "Redefining Security," *Foreign Affairs*, vol 68, no 2, Spring 1989, pp 162–77.

7. Susanne Schmeidl, "(Human) Security Dilemmas: Long-Term Implications of the Afghan Refugee Crisis," *Third World Quarterly*, vol 23, no 1, 2002, pp 7–29.

8. See Kanti Bajpai, "The Idea of Human Security," *International Studies*, vol 40, no 3, July–September 2003, pp 195–228 at pp 203–04.

9. For an elaboration of this approach, see Andrew Mack (ed.), *Human Security Report 2005: War and Peace in the 21st Century* (Oxford: Oxford University Press, 2005).

10. Thomas Hobbes, *Leviathan* (Cambridge: Cambridge University Press, 1996), pp 88–89.

11. Max Weber, *Economy and Society: An Outline of Interpretive Sociology* (Berkeley & Los Angeles, CA: University of California Press, 1978), vol I, p 56.

12. These categories are outlined in Dylan Hendrickson and Andrzej Karkoszka, "Security Sector Reform and Donor Policies," in Albrecht Schnabel and Hans-Georg Ehrhart (eds), *Security Sector Reform and Post-Conflict Peacebuilding* (Tokyo: United Nations University Press, 2005), pp 19–44 at p 23.

13. See Christopher Kinsey, "Challenging International Law: A Dilemma of Private Security Companies," *Conflict, Security and Development*, vol 5, no 3, December 2005, pp 269–93.

14. See William Maley, "International Force and Political Reconstruction: Cambodia, East Timor and Afghanistan," in Albrecht Schnabel and Hans-Georg Ehrhart (eds), *Security Sector Reform and Post-Conflict Peacebuilding* (Tokyo: United Nations University Press, 2005), pp 297–312.

15. See Mark Sedra, "Security Sector Reform in Afghanistan: The Slide Towards Expediency," *International Peacekeeping*, vol 13, no 1, March 2006, pp 94–110.

16. Eric Scheye and Gordon Peake, "To Arrest Insecurity: Time for a Revised Security Sector Reform Agenda," *Conflict, Security and Development*, vol 5, no 3, December 2005, pp 295–327.

17. Kenneth Katzman, *Afghanistan: Post-War Governance, Security, and U.S. Policy* (Washington DC: Congressional Research Service, The Library of Congress, May 19, 2005), p 25.

18. See Zahid Hussain, "Taleban 'Preparing for Spring Attacks'," *Times*, 29 March 2002. On Operation Anaconda, see Anthony H. Cordesman, *The Lessons of Afghanistan: War Fighting, Intelligence, and Force Transformation* (Washington DC: Centre for Strategic and International Studies, 2002), pp 63–76; Sean Naylor, *Not a Good Day to Die: The Untold Story of Operation Anaconda* (New York: Berkley Books, 2005).

19. On the murder of Ricardo Munguia, see William Maley, "The 'War Against Terrorism' in South Asia," *Contemporary South Asia*, vol 12, no 2, June 2003, pp 203–17 at p 214. For discussion of subsequent violence, see

Michael Bhatia, Kevin Lanigan and Philip Wilkinson, *Minimal Investments, Minimal Results: The Failure of Security Policy in Afghanistan* (Kabul: Afghanistan Research and Evaluation Unit, June 2004), pp 4–8.

20. Declan Walsh and Bazargai Saidan, "Across the Border from Britain's Troops, Taliban Rises Again," *Guardian*, 27 May 2006.

21. See Tim Judah, "The Taliban Papers," *Survival*, vol 44, no 1, 2002, pp 8–80; Mariam Abou Zahab and Olivier Roy, *Islamist Networks: The Afghan–Pakistan Connection* (London: Hurst & Co., 2004); and Daniel Byman, *Deadly Connections: States that Sponsor Terrorism* (Cambridge: Cambridge University Press, 2005), pp 187–218.

22. See International Crisis Group, *Unfulfilled Promises: Pakistan's Failure to Tackle Extremism* (Brussels: ICG Asia Report no 73, 16 January 2004); and International Crisis Group, *The State of Sectarianism in Pakistan* (Brussels: ICG Asia Report no 95, 18 April 2005).

23. Carlotta Gall, "Pakistan Allows Taliban to Train, a Detained Fighter Says," *New York Times*, 4 August 2004.

24. See David Rohde, "Pakistan Vows to Stop Taliban; Westerners Just Scoff," *New York Times*, 24 August 2004.

25. See International Crisis Group, *Afghanistan: The Problem of Pashtun Alienation* (Brussels: ICG Asia Report no 62, 5 August 2003), pp 20–22.

26. See David Montero, "Corruption Eroding Afghan security," *Christian Science Monitor*, 28 April 2006.

27. On the prevalence of this phenomenon in Kandahar, see Sarah Chayes, "Afghanistan: The Night Fairies," *Bulletin of the Atomic Scientists*, vol 62, no 2, March–April 2006, pp 17–19.

28. On Pushtunistan, see Rajat Ganguly, *Kin State Intervention in Ethnic Conflicts: Lessons from South Asia* (New Delhi: SAGE Publications, 1998), pp 162–92.

29. See Frédéric Grare, *Pakistan: The Resurgence of Baluch Nationalism* (Washington DC: Carnegie Papers no 65, Carnegie Endowment for International Peace, January 2006); Carlotta Gall, "In Remote Pakistan Province, a Civil War Festers," *New York Times*, 2 April 2006.

30. See Barnett R. Rubin, "The Flash Point Where Afghanistan Meets Pakistan," *International Herald Tribune*, 12 January 2004; Amin Saikal, "Securing Afghanistan's Border," *Survival*, vol 48, no 1, Spring 2006, pp 129–42.

31. For a discussion of these problems, see Barnett R. Rubin, Ashraf Ghani,

William Maley, Ahmed Rashid, and Olivier Roy, *Afghanistan: Reconstruction and Peacebuilding in a Regional Framework* (Bern: KOFF Peacebuilding Reports 1/2001, Swiss Peace Foundation, 2001).

32. See *Paying for the Taliban's Crimes: Abuses Against Ethnic Pashtuns in Northern Afghanistan* (New York: Human Rights Watch, April 2002).

33. For background, see *Afghanistan: The Problem of Pashtun Alienation*, pp 14–19.

34. Louise I. Shelley, "Transnational Organized Crime: An Imminent Threat to the Nation-State?," *Journal of International Affairs*, vol 48, no 2, Winter 1995, pp 463–89 at p 464.

35. Phil Williams, "Transnational Criminal Organizations: Strategic Alliances," *Washington Quarterly*, vol 18, no 1, Winter 1995, pp 57–72.

36. Matt Weiner, *An Afghan "Narco-State"? Dynamics, Assessment and Security Implications of the Afghan Opium Industry* (Canberra: Canberra Papers on Strategy and Defence no 158, Strategic and Defence Studies Centre, Australian National University, 2004), p 18. See also Alain Labrousse, *Afghanistan: Opium de Guerre, Opium de Paix* (Paris: Éditions Mille et Une Nuits, 2005).

37. This has prompted a debate on the utility of such an "Afghan model" for other theatres of combat. See Richard B. Andres, Craig Wills and Thomas Griffith Jr, "Winning with Allies: The Strategic Value of the Afghan Model," *International Security*, vol 30, no 3, Winter 2005–06, pp 124–60; and Stephen D. Biddle, "Allies, Airpower, and Modern Warfare: The Afghan Model in Afghanistan and Iraq," *International Security*, vol 30, no 3, Winter 2005–06, pp 161–76.

38. Larry Goodson, *Security in Afghanistan: The Continuing Challenge* (Washington DC: Center for American Progress, 2004), p 13 fn 4. For a depiction of US forces in action in Afghanistan, see Robert D. Kaplan, *Imperial Grunts: The American Military on the Ground* (New York: Random House, 2005), pp 185–255.

39. Katzman, *Afghanistan: Post-War Governance, Security, and U.S. Policy*, p 26.

40. For more detailed discussion of ISAF, see Amin Saikal, "Afghanistan's Transition: ISAF's Stabilisation Role?," *Third World Quarterly*, vol 27, no 3, 2006, pp 525–34.

41. Alan Sipress, "Peacekeepers Won't Go Beyond Kabul, Cheney Says," *Washington Post*, 20 March 2002.

42. See *Afghanistan: Are We Losing the Peace?* (New York: Chairman's Report of an Independent Task Force Cosponsored by the Council on Foreign Relations and the Asia Society, Council on Foreign Relations, June 2003), p 9.

43. See Philip H. Gordon, "Back Up NATO's Afghanistan Force," *International Herald Tribune*, 8 January 2006.

44. See Frederick M. Burkle, Jr, "Complex Emergencies and Military Capabilities," in William Maley, Charles Sampford and Ramesh Thakur (eds), *From Civil Strife to Civil Society: Civil and Military Responsibilities in Disrupted States* (Tokyo: United Nations University Press, 2003), pp 96–108.

45. Michael J. Dziedzic and Colonel Michael K. Seidl, *Provincial Reconstruction Teams and Military Relations with International and Nongovernmental Organizations in Afghanistan* (Washington DC: Special Report no 147, United States Institute of Peace, September 2005), p 6.

46. See Barbara J. Stapleton, "Civil Society Perspectives on the Role of PRTs," PRT "Best Practices" Conference, NATO Headquarters, Brussels, 28–29 November 2005.

47. M. Nazif Shahrani, "The Future of the State and the Structure of Community Governance in Afghanistan," in William Maley (ed.), *Fundamentalism Reborn? Afghanistan and the Taliban* (London: Hurst & Co., 1998), pp 212–42 at p 238.

48. Samuel M. Makinda, "Disarmament and Reintegration of Combatants," in William Maley, Charles Sampford and Ramesh Thakur (eds), *From Civil Strife to Civil Society: Civil and Military Responsibilities in Disrupted States* (Tokyo: United Nations University Press, 2003), pp 309–26 at pp 322–23.

49. See Alpaslan Özerdem, "Disarmament, Demobilisation and Reintegration of Former Combatants in Afghanistan: Lessons Learned from a Cross-Cultural Perspective," *Third World Quarterly*, vol 23, no 5, 2002, pp 961–75.

50. *Afghanistan's New Beginnings Project: Fact Sheet* (Kabul: ANBP/United Nations Development Program, August 2005).

51. See International Crisis Group, *Disarmament and Reintegration in Afghanistan* (Brussels: ICG Asia Report no 65, 30 September 2003).

52. See International Crisis Group, *Afghanistan: Getting Disarmament Back on Track* (Kabul/Brussels: ICG Asia Briefing no 35, 23 February 2005), p 2.

53. See Christian Dennys, *Disarmament, Demobilization and Rearmament?*

The Effects of Disarmament in Afghanistan (Kabul: Occasional Paper, Japan Afghan NGO Network, 6 June 2005).

54. See *Afghanistan National Development Strategy: An Interim Strategy for Security, Governance, Economic Growth and Poverty Reduction* (Kabul: Islamic Republic of Afghanistan, 2006), p 121.

55. See Ali A. Jalali, "Rebuilding Afghanistan's National Army," *Parameters*, vol 32, no 3, Autumn 2002, pp 72–86.

56. *Afghanistan: Managing Public Finances for Development* (Washington DC: The World Bank, Report no 34582–AF, 22 Dec 2005), vol I, p 98.

57. Barnett R. Rubin, "Constructing Sovereignty for Security," *Survival*, vol 7, no 4, Winter 2005, pp 93–106 at p 99.

58. Richard M. Pfeffer (ed.), *No More Vietnams? The War and the Future of American Foreign Policy* (New York: Harper & Row, 1968), p 163.

59. Mark Lander, "Afghan Plan a New Army of 70,000," *New York Times*, 3 December 2002.

60. Sedra, "Security Sector Reform in Afghanistan: The Slide Towards Expediency," p 97.

61. Scott Baldrauf, "A 'Half Full' Afghan Army," *Christian Science Monitor*, 10 February 2006.

62. *Afghanistan: Managing Public Finances for Development*, vol I, p 21.

63. Sedra, "Security Sector Reform in Afghanistan: The Slide Towards Expediency," p 97.

64. See Thomas E. Ricks, "Iraqi Battalion Refuses to 'Fight Iraqis,'" *Washington Post*, 11 April 2004.

65. Alice E. Hills, "The Policing of Fragmented States," *Low Intensity Conflict and Law Enforcement*, vol 5, no 3, Winter 1996, pp 334–54 at p 335.

66. These are elaborated in John McFarlane and William Maley, "Civilian Police in UN Peace Operations: Some Lessons from Recent Australian Experience," in Ramesh Thakur and Albrecht Schnabel (eds), *United Nations Peacekeeping Operations: Ad Hoc Missions, Permanent Engagement* (Tokyo: United Nations University Press, 2001), pp 182–211 at pp 186–187.

67. See Amnesty International, *Afghanistan: Police Reconstruction Essential for the Protection of Human Rights* (London, Amnesty International, ASA 11/003/2003, March 2003), p 12.

68. On political police, see Amos Perlmutter, *Modern Authoritarianism: A Comparative Institutional Analysis* (New Haven: Yale University Press,

1981), pp 35–36. On the communist secret police in Afghanistan, see William Maley, *The Afghanistan Wars* (New York: Palgrave Macmillan, 2002), pp 97–102.

69. Sedra, "Security Sector Reform in Afghanistan: The Slide Towards Expediency," p 98.

70. Rama Mani, *Ending Impunity and Building Justice in Afghanistan* (Kabul: Afghanistan Research and Evaluation Unit, December 2003), p 18. See also *Afghanistan: Reject Known Abusers as Police Chiefs* (New York: Human Rights Watch, 4 May 2006).

71. *Afghanistan: Managing Public Finances for Development*, vol I, p 21.

72. Quoted in Bhatia, Lanigan and Wilkinson, *Minimal Investments, Minimal Results: The Failure of Security Policy in Afghanistan*, p 17.

73. See *Afghanistan Security: Efforts to Establish Army and Police Have Made Progress, but Future Plans Need to Be Better Defined* (Washington DC: Report to the Committee on International Relations, House of Representatives, GAO–05–575, United States Government Accountability Office, June 2005), p 23.

74. See Condoleezza Rice, "The Military under Democracy," *Journal of Democracy*, vol 3, no 2, April 1992, pp 27–42 at pp 36–38.

75. Rubin, "Constructing Sovereignty for Security," p 99.

76. See Michael W. Jackson, *Matters of Justice* (London: Croom Helm, 1986), pp 104–08.

77. Pamela Constable, "Afghan Office of U.S. Firm Hit by Bomb," *Washington Post*, 30 August 2004.

78. Carlotta Gall, "Mercenaries in Afghan Case Get 8 to 10 Years in Prison," *New York Times*, 16 September 2004.

79. For an extended discussion of this topic, see Deborah D. Avant, *The Market for Force: The Consequences of Privatizing Security* (Cambridge: Cambridge University Press, 2005).

80. *Dateline*, SBS Television (Australia), 19 October 2005.

4. Promoting human development

1. See *Afghanistan: National Human Development Report 2004. Security with a Human Face: Challenges and Responsibilities* (Kabul: United Nations Development Programme, 2004), pp 275–82 (Annexure 3).

2. *Afghanistan: State Building, Sustaining Growth, and Reducing Poverty* (Washington DC: The World Bank, 2005), p 5.

3. Sippi Azarbaijani-Moghaddam, "Afghan Women on the Margins of the Twenty-First Century," in Antonio Donini, Norah Niland and Karin Wermester (eds), *Nation-Building Unraveled? Aid, Peace and Justice in Afghanistan* (Bloomfield: Kumarian Press, 2004), pp 95–113 at p 101. She goes on to argue that "RAWA has as yet to prove that its relentless self-promotion has contributed in any significant way to the betterment of Afghan women" (p 101), and states that "The author's recent guided tour of 'secret' RAWA projects in Kabul provided ample evidence of the group's painstaking charades aimed at manipulating, misinforming, and giving anything but the right impressions regarding the reality of life for ordinary Afghan women" (p 113, fn 18).

4. See William Maley, "Women and Public Policy in Afghanistan: A Comment," *World Development*, vol 24, no 1, January 1996, pp 203–06.

5. See William Maley, "Realising the Minimal State: The Case of Afghanistan," *Agenda*, vol 3, no 2, 1996, pp 261–64.

6. Richard Rose, "Toward a Civil Economy," *Journal of Democracy*, vol 3, no 2, April 1992, pp 13–26.

7. See Liz Alden Wily, *Land Rights in Crisis: Restoring Tenure Security in Afghanistan* (Kabul: Afghanistan Research and Evaluation Unit, March 2003), pp 3–4.

8. *Afghanistan: National Human Development Report 2004. Security with a Human Face: Challenges and Responsibilities*, p 276.

9. See Jo Beall and Daniel Esser, *Shaping Urban Futures: Challenges to Governing and Managing Afghan Cities* (Kabul: Afghanistan Research and Evaluation Unit, March 2005), p 11.

10. Ibid, pp 33–35.

11. For the full text, see *International Journal of Refugee Law*, vol 10, no 3, July 1998, pp 586–92.

12. Ronald Waldman and Homaira Hanif, *The Public Health System in Afghanistan* (Kabul: Afghanistan Research and Evaluation Unit, May–June 2002), p 1.

13. *Afghanistan: National Human Development Report 2004. Security with a Human Face: Challenges and Responsibilities*, p 27.

14. Ibid, p 278.

15. Ibid, p 28.

16. *Afghanistan: Managing Public Finances for Development* (Washington DC: The World Bank, Report no 34582–AF, 22 Dec 2005), vol IV, p 24.

17. Maxwell J. Fry, *The Afghan Economy: Money, Finance and the Critical Constraints to Economic Development* (Leiden: E. J. Brill, 1974), p 14.

18. Abdul Wasay Najimi, *Report on a Survey on SCA Supported Girls' Education and SCA Built School Buildings in Afghanistan in Regions under Southern and Eastern SCA Regional Management* (Peshawar: Education Technical Support Unit, Swedish Committee for Afghanistan, 29 August 1997).

19. Seth G. Jones, Lee H. Hilborne, C. Ross Anthony, Lois M. Davis, Federico Girosi, Cheryl Benard, Rachel M. Schwanger, Anita Datar Garten and Anga Timilsina, *Securing Health: Lessons from Nation-Building Missions* (Santa Monica: RAND Center for Domestic and International Health Security, 2006), p 219.

20. See Amartya Sen, *Development as Freedom* (New York: Random House, 1999), pp 195–98.

21. See Robin Jeffrey, "Legacies of Matriliny: The Place of Women and the 'Kerala Model,'" *Pacific Affairs*, vol 77, no 4, 2004–05, pp 647–64.

22. See Pamela Hunte, *Looking Beyond the School Walls: Household Decision-Making and School Enrolment in Afghanistan* (Kabul: Afghanistan Research and Evaluation Unit, March 2006), p 3.

23. See *Afghanistan: National Reconstruction and Poverty Reduction: The Role of Women in Afghanistan's Future* (Washington DC: The World Bank, March 2005), pp 100–01.

24. See, for example, Ashraf Ghani, "Islam and State-Building in a Tribal Society: Afghanistan 1880–1901," *Modern Asian Studies*, vol 12, no 2, 1978, pp 269–84; Ashraf Ghani, "Afghanistan: Administration," in Ehsan Yarshater (ed.), *Encyclopædia Iranica* (London: Routledge & Kegan Paul, 1985), vol I, pp 558–64; and Ashraf Ghani, "The Afghan State and Its Adaptation to the Environment of Central and Southwest Asia," in Hafeez Malik (ed.), *Soviet–American Relations with Pakistan, Iran and Afghanistan* (London: Macmillan, 1987), pp 310–32.

25. Michael Carnahan, "Next Steps in Reforming the Ministry of Finance," in Michael Carnahan, Nick Manning, Richard Bontjer and Stéphane Guimbert (eds), *Reforming Fiscal and Economic Management in Afghanistan* (Washington DC: The World Bank, 2004), pp 123–49 at p 123.

26. Ibid, p 146.

27. *Afghanistan: Managing Public Finances for Development*, vol I, p 10.

28. Ibid, p 14.

29. Ibid, p 32.

30. Ibid, p 33.

31. Ibid, p 53.

32. *Afghanistan: State Building, Sustaining Growth, and Reducing Poverty*, p 51.

33. See Aron Katsenelinboigen, "Coloured Markets in the Soviet Union," *Soviet Studies*, vol 29, no 1, January 1977, pp 62–85.

34. Conrad Schetter, "The 'Bazaar Economy' of Afghanistan," in Christine Noelle-Karimi, Conrad Schetter and Reinhard Schlagintweit (eds), *Afghanistan: A Country without a State?* (Frankfurt am Main: IKO-Verlag für Interkulturelle Kommunikation, 2002), pp 109–27 at p 115.

35. For varying perspectives, see F. A. Hayek, *Individualism and Economic Order* (Chicago: University of Chicago Press, 1948), and James C. Scott, *Seeing Like a State: How Certain Schemes to Improve the Human Condition Have Failed* (New Haven: Yale University Press, 1998).

36. See William J. Baumol, *The Free-Market Innovation Machine: Analyzing the Growth Miracle of Capitalism* (Princeton: Princeton University Press, 2002).

37. Jonathan Goodhand, "Afghanistan," in Michael Pugh and Neil Cooper with Jonathan Goodhand, *War Economies in a Regional Context: Challenges of Transformation* (Boulder: Lynne Rienner, 2004), pp 45–89 at pp 63–65.

38. See Sarah Lister and Adam Pain, *Trading in Power: The Politics of "Free" Markets in Afghanistan* (Kabul: Afghanistan Research and Evaluation Unit, June 2004).

39. On these cases, see Andrew MacIntyre, *Business and Politics in Indonesia* (Sydney: Allen & Unwin, 1991); Andrew MacIntyre (ed.), *Business and Government in Industrialising Asia* (Ithaca: Cornell University Press, 1994); and Peter Searle, *The Riddle of Malaysian Capitalism: Rent-Seekers or Real Capitalists?* (Honolulu: University of Hawai'i Press, 1999).

40. See Phil Reeves, "Afghan Elite Seizes Land for Mansions as Poor Lose Homes," *Independent*, 19 September 2003; Griff Witte, "In Kabul, a Stark Gulf Between Wealthy Few and the Poor," *Washington Post*, 9 December 2005.

41. *The Investment Climate in Afghanistan: Exploiting Opportunities in an Uncertain Environment* (Washington DC: Finance and Private Sector Development Unit, South Asia Region, The World Bank, December 2005), pp 21–24, 40–44.

42. See Samuel Munzele Maimbo, *The Money Exchange Dealers of Kabul: A Study of the Hawala System in Afghanistan* (Washington DC: World Bank Working Paper no 13, The World Bank, 2003).

43. See Jon W. Anderson, "There Are No Khans Anymore: Economic Development and Social Change in Tribal Afghanistan," *Middle East Journal*, vol 32, no 2, Spring 1978, pp 167–83.

44. See Ruxandra Boros, "Microcredit in Afghanistan: Challenges and Opportunities," *Afghanistan Info*, no 57, September 2005, pp 11–12.

45. *Afghanistan: State Building, Sustaining Growth, and Reducing Poverty*, p 71.

46. For a classic examination of this phenomenon, see Milton Friedman (ed.), *Studies in the Quantity Theory of Money* (Chicago: University of Chicago Press, 1956).

47. *Afghanistan: State Building, Sustaining Growth, and Reducing Poverty*, p 5.

48. Christopher Ward and William Byrd, *Afghanistan's Opium Drug Economy* (Washington DC: Working Paper SASPR–5, The World Bank, December 2004), pp 9–10.

49. *Afghanistan Opium Survey 2005* (Kabul: United Nations Office on Drugs and Crime and Government of Afghanistan Ministry of Counter Narcotics, November 2005), p 5.

50. Ibid, p 1.

51. "Afghan Government and United Nations Announce Results of First National Survey on Drug Use in Afghanistan" (Kabul: Press Release, United Nations Office on Drugs and Crime and Government of Afghanistan Ministry of Counter Narcotics, 24 November 2005).

52. *Afghanistan: State Building, Sustaining Growth, and Reducing Poverty*, pp 118–19.

53. For a comprehensive overview, see William B. McAllister, *Drug Diplomacy in the Twentieth Century: An International History* (London: Routledge, 2000). Article 7 of the Afghan constitution also contains a prohibition on "intoxicants" (*muskirat*). In the eyes of many Afghans, alcohol and alcoholism pose greater threats to social stability than do opiates. See Ralph Seccombe, "Squeezing the Balloon: International Drugs Policy," *Drug and Alcohol Review*, vol 14, 1995, pp 311–16.

54. See Ralph Seccombe, "Troublesome Boomerang: Illicit Drug Policy and Security," *Security Dialogue*, vol 28, no 3, 1997, pp 287–99.

55. James Risen, *State of War: The Secret History of the CIA and the Bush Administration* (New York: Free Press, 2006), pp 159–60.

56. See Barnett R. Rubin, *Road to Ruin: Afghanistan's Booming Opium Industry* (Washington DC: Center for American Progress, 7 October 2004), pp 15–16; Barnett R. Rubin and Omar Zakhilwal, "A War on Drugs, or a War on Farmers?," *Wall Street Journal*, 14 January 2005.

57. *Afghanistan: State Building, Sustaining Growth, and Reducing Poverty*, p 120.

58. See Barnett R. Rubin, *Afghanistan's Uncertain Transition from Turmoil to Normalcy* (New York: Council Special Report no 12, Council on Foreign Relations, March 2006), p 34.

59. See David Mansfield and Adam Pain, *Alternative Livelihoods: Substance or Slogan?* (Kabul: Afghanistan Research and Evaluation Unit, October 2005); and also Adam Pain and Sue Lautze, *Addressing Livelihoods in Afghanistan* (Kabul: Afghanistan Research and Evaluation Unit, September 2002).

60. Jaghori Hazaras have a long history of sophisticated money dealings: see Alessandro Monsutti, *War and Migration: Social Networks and Economic Strategies of the Hazaras of Afghanistan* (New York: Routledge, 2005), pp 173–205.

61. See William Maley, "Security, People Smuggling, and Australia's New Afghan Refugees," *Australian Journal of International Affairs*, vol 55, no 3, 2001, pp 351–70; and Michael Gordon, *Freeing Ali: The Human Face of the Pacific Solution* (Sydney: UNSW Press, 2005).

62. Hernando de Soto, *The Mystery of Capital: Why Capitalism Triumphs in the West and Fails Everywhere Else* (London: Black Swan, 2001), p 241.

63. Carol J. Riphenburg, "Afghanistan: Out of the Globalisation Mainstream?," *Third World Quarterly*, vol 27, no 3, 2006, pp 507–24 at p 518.

64. For a discussion of this important issue, see Mark P. Thirlwell, *India: The Next Economic Giant* (Sydney: Lowy Institute Paper 01, Lowy Institute for International Policy, 2004).

65. See Robert L. Canfield, "Restructuring in Greater Central Asia: Changing Political Configurations," *Asian Survey*, vol 32, no 10, October 1992, pp 875–87.

66. On the negative effects of the Afghanistan situation on Central Asia, see Paula R. Newberg, "Surviving State Failure: Internal War and Regional Conflict in Afghanistan's Neighborhood," in Cynthia J. Arnson and

I. William Zartman (eds), *Rethinking the Economics of War: The Intersection of Need, Creed, and Greed* (Washington DC: Woodrow Wilson Center Press, 2005), pp 206–33 at pp 223–25.

67. See William Maley, *The Foreign Policy of the Taliban* (New York: Council on Foreign Relations, 2000), pp 15–16.

68. *Afghanistan: National Human Development Report 2004. Security with a Human Face: Challenges and Responsibilities*, p 198.

69. Amin Saikal, in *The Rise and Fall of the Shah* (Princeton: Princeton University Press, 1980) has demonstrated very effectively that while the Shah made a concerted push in his later years to achieve regional domination, he was unable ultimately to overcome the burden of his perceived dependence on the United States.

70. For a poignant discussion of this problem, see Ann Jones, *Kabul in Winter: Life without Peace in Afghanistan* (New York: Metropolitan Books, 2006), pp 280–85.

71. William Maley and Fazel Haq Saikal, *Political Order in Post-Communist Afghanistan* (Boulder: Lynne Rienner, 1992), p 56.

72. See *Afghanistan Reconstruction: Deteriorating Security and Limited Resources Have Impeded Progress; Improvements in U.S. Strategy Needed* (Washington DC: Report to Congressional Committees, GAO–04–403, United States General Accounting Office, June 2004), p 10.

73. Joe Stephens and David B. Ottaway, "A Rebuilding Plan Full of Cracks," *Washington Post*, 20 November 2005.

74. *Afghanistan Aid Flows as of November 2003* (New York: Center on International Cooperation, New York University, 2003).

75. Fariba Nawa, *Afghanistan, Inc.: A CorpWatch Investigative Report* (Oakland: CorpWatch, 2006).

76. See Richard Beeston, "Good Times Roll in City Where Fun Was Banned," *The Times*, 15 March 2006.

77. For a less populist example of his thinking, see Ramazan Bachardoust, *Afghanistan: Droit Constitutionnel, Histoire, Régimes Politiques et Relations Diplomatiques Depuis 1747* (Paris: L'Harmattan, 2002).

78. See Antonio Donini, "Principles, Politics, and Pragmatism in the International Response to the Afghan Crisis," in Antonio Donini, Norah Niland and Karin Wermester (eds), *Nation-Building Unraveled? Aid, Peace and Justice in Afghanistan* (Bloomfield: Kumarian Press, 2004), pp 117–42; and Antonio Donini, "An Elusive Quest: Integration in the Response to the

Afghan Crisis," *Ethics and International Affairs*, vol 18, no 2, 2004, pp 21–27.

79. David Rieff, *A Bed for the Night: Humanitarianism in Crisis* (New York: Simon & Schuster, 2002), p 265.

5. Afghanistan and the world

1. See Gerry Simpson, *Great Powers and Outlaw States: Unequal Sovereigns in the International Legal Order* (Cambridge: Cambridge University Press, 2004), pp 319–51.

2. Associated Press, 28 April 2006.

3. Zalmay Khalilzad, "How to Nation-Build: Ten Lessons from Afghanistan," *National Interest*, no 80, Summer 2005, pp 19–27 at p 1.

4. See Pamela Constable, "U.S. Commander in Afghanistan Thinks Locally," *Washington Post*, 4 May 2006.

5. Quoted in N. C. Aizenman, "Karzai Seeks Long-Term U.S. Security Deal," *Washington Post*, 13 April 2005.

6. "Joint Declaration of the United States–Afghanistan Strategic Partnership" (Washington DC: White House Press Release, Office of the Press Secretary, 23 May 2005).

7. See Adam Garfinkle, "Afghanistanding," *Orbis*, vol 43, no 3, Summer 1999, pp 405–18.

8. See *The Road to Abu Ghraib* (New York: Human Rights Watch, 2004); Mark Danner, *Torture and Truth: America, Abu Ghraib, and the War on Terror* (New York: New York Review of Books, 2004).

9. See Tim Golden, "In U.S. Report, Brutal Details of 2 Afghan Inmates' Deaths," *New York Times*, 20 May 2005.

10. *By the Numbers: Findings of the Detainee Abuse and Accountability Project* (New York: Human Rights Watch, April 2006), p 6.

11. Robert Cryer, "The Fine Art of Friendship: Jus in Bello in Afghanistan," *Journal of Conflict and Security Law*, vol 7, no 1, April 2002, pp 37–83 at p 83.

12. See Marvin G. Weinbaum, *Pakistan and Afghanistan: Resistance and Reconstruction* (Boulder: Westview Press, 1994).

13. See Shirin Tahir-Kheli, *The United States and Pakistan: The Evolution of an Influence Relationship* (New York: Praeger, 1982); Dennis Kux, *The United States and Pakistan, 1947–2000: Disenchanted Allies* (Baltimore: Woodrow Wilson Center Press, 2001).

14. On Pakistan's difficulties, see generally Owen Bennett Jones, *Pakistan: Eye of the Storm* (New Haven: Yale University Press, 2002); Stephen Philip Cohen, *The Idea of Pakistan* (Washington DC: Brookings Institution Press, 2004); and Husain Haqqani, *Pakistan: Between Mosque and Military* (Washington DC: Carnegie Endowment for International Peace, 2005).

15. See Thomas Perry Thornton, "Pakistan: Fifty Years of Insecurity," in Selig S. Harrison, Paul H. Kreisberg, and Dennis Kux (eds), *India and Pakistan: The First Fifty Years* (Cambridge: Cambridge University Press, 1999), pp 170–88.

16. See William Maley, "Talibanisation and Pakistan," in *Talibanisation: Extremism and Regional Instability in South and Central Asia* (Berlin: Conflict Prevention Network: Stiftung Wissenschaft und Politik, 2001), pp 53–74.

17. On the Kashmir issue, see Sumit Ganguly, *The Crisis in Kashmir: Portents of War, Hopes of Peace* (Cambridge: Cambridge University Press, 1997); Sumit Ganguly, *Conflict Unending: India–Pakistan Tensions since 1947* (New York: Columbia University Press, 2001); Sumantra Bose, *Kashmir: Roots of Conflict, Paths to Peace* (Cambridge: Harvard University Press, 2003).

18. See David Montero, "Iran, US Share Afghan Goals," *Christian Science Monitor*, 4 May 2006; Mohsen M. Milani, "Iran's Policy Towards Afghanistan," *Middle East Journal*, vol 60, no 2, Spring 2006, pp 235–56.

19. See Amin Saikal, *Islam and the West: Conflict or Cooperation?* (New York: Palgrave Macmillan, 2003), p 88.

20. See Amin Saikal, "The Regional Politics of the Afghan Crisis," in Amin Saikal and William Maley (eds), *The Soviet Withdrawal from Afghanistan* (Cambridge: Cambridge University Press, 1989), pp 52–66 at pp 56–57.

21. See Neelesh Misra, *173 Hours in Captivity: The Hijacking of IC814* (New Delhi: HarperCollins, 2000), p 174.

22. See William Maley, "The UN and Afghanistan: 'Doing Its Best' or 'Failure of a Mission'?," in William Maley (ed.), *Fundamentalism Reborn? Afghanistan and the Taliban* (London: Hurst & Co., 1998), pp 182–98.

23. *Afghanistan: National Human Development Report 2004. Security with a Human Face: Challenges and Responsibilities* (Kabul: United Nations Development Programme, 2004), p 214.

24. *The Situation in Afghanistan and its Implications for International Peace and Security: Report of the Secretary-General* (New York: United Nations, A/56/681, S/2001/1157, 6 December 2001), para 2.

25. See *Report of the Panel on United Nations Peace Operations* (New York: United Nations, A/55/305, S/2000/809, 21 August 2000).

26. *The Situation in Afghanistan and Its Implications for International Peace and Security: Report of the Secretary-General* (New York: United Nations: A/56/875, S/2002/278, 18 March 2002), para 98.

27. Richard Caplan, *International Governance of War-Torn Territories: Rule and Reconstruction* (Oxford: Oxford University Press, 2005), p 14, fn 32.

28. Nicholas Stockton, *Strategic Coordination in Afghanistan* (Kabul: Afghanistan Research and Evaluation Unit, August 2002), p 47.

29. Chris Johnson and Jolyon Leslie, *Afghanistan: The Mirage of Peace* (London: Zed Books, 2004), p 200. See also Norah Niland, "Justice Postponed: The Marginalization of Human Rights in Afghanistan," in Antonio Donini, Norah Niland and Karin Wermester (eds), *Nation-Building Unraveled? Aid, Peace and Justice in Afghanistan* (Bloomfield: Kumarian Press, 2004), pp 61–82.

30. See Simon Chesterman, *You, the People: The United Nations, Transitional Administration, and State-Building* (Oxford: Oxford University Press, 2004), p 90.

31. On Islamic ideas about territorial states, see James P. Piscatori, *Islam in a World of Nation-States* (Cambridge: Cambridge University Press, 1986). For a critical discussion of western thinking, see Stephen D. Krasner, *Sovereignty: Organized Hypocrisy* (Princeton: Princeton University Press, 1999).

32. See Khaled Abou El Fadl, *The Great Theft: Wrestling Islam from the Extremists* (San Francisco: HarperCollins, 2005).

33. See Olivier Roy, *Globalised Islam: The Search for a New Ummah* (London: Hurst & Co., 2004), p 55.

34. *International Herald Tribune*, 22 April 1992.

35. See Fawaz A. Gerges, *The Far Enemy: Why Jihad Went Global* (Cambridge: Cambridge University Press, 2005), pp 185–250.

36. See Louis Dupree, "Myth and Reality in Afghan 'Neutralism,'" *Central Asian Survey*, vol 7, nos 2–3, 1988, pp 145–51.

37. See Sumit Ganguly and Devin T. Hegarty, *Fearful Symmetry: India–Pakistan Crises in the Shadow of Nuclear Weapons* (Seattle: University of Washington Press, 2005).

38. Barnett R. Rubin, *Afghanistan's Uncertain Transition from Turmoil to Normalcy* (New York: Council Special Report no 12, Council on Foreign Relations, March 2006), p 14.

39. For some examples of this from the 1980s, see William Maley, "Political Legitimation in Contemporary Afghanistan," *Asian Survey*, vol 37, no 6, June 1987, pp 705–25.

40. See Michael Scheuer, *Imperial Hubris: Why the West is Losing the War on Terror* (Washington DC: Potomac Books, 2005), pp 226–30; Anatol Lieven, *America Right or Wrong: An Anatomy of American Nationalism* (New York: Oxford University Press, 2005), pp 173–216; Stephen M. Walt, *Taming American Power: The Global Response to U.S. Primacy* (New York: W. W. Norton, 2005), pp 200–10; and most recently, John J. Mearsheimer and Stephen M. Walt, *The Israel Lobby and U.S. Foreign Policy* (Cambridge: John F. Kennedy School of Government Faculty Research Working Paper no RWP06–011, Harvard University, March 2006).

6. Whither Afghanistan?

1. "The Failed States Index," *Foreign Policy*, May–June 2006, pp 50–58.

2. See Micheline R. Ishay, *The History of Human Rights: From Ancient Times to the Globalization Era* (Berkeley & Los Angeles: University of California Press, 2004).

3. For a detailed discussion, see W. Michael Reisman and James Silk, "Which Law Applies to the Afghan Conflict?," *American Journal of International Law*, vol 82, no 3, 1988, pp 459–86.

4. For a comprehensive overview, see *Casting Shadows: War Crimes and Crimes against Humanity 1978–2001* (Kabul: Afghanistan Justice Project, 2005).

5. See Jeri Laber and Barnett R. Rubin, *"A Nation Is Dying": Afghanistan under the Soviet 1979–87* (Evanston: Northwestern University Press, 1988).

6. See *Blood-Stained Hands: Past Atrocities in Kabul and Afghanistan's Legacy of Impunity* (New York: Human Rights Watch, 2005).

7. See *Afghanistan: The Massacre in Mazar-i Sharif* (New York: Human Rights Watch, 1998).

8. See Norah Niland, "Justice Postponed: The Marginalization of Human Rights in Afghanistan," in Antonio Donini, Norah Niland and Karin Wermester (eds), *Nation-Building Unraveled? Aid, Peace and Justice in Afghanistan* (Bloomfield: Kumarian Press, 2004), pp 61–82.

9. Helen Durham, "Mercy and Justice in the Transition Period," in William Maley, Charles Sampford and Ramesh Thakur (eds), *From Civil Strife to Civil Society: Civil and Military Responsibilities in Disrupted States* (Tokyo: United Nations University Press, 2003), pp 145–60 at p 147.

10. On Nuremberg, see Telford Taylor, *The Anatomy of the Nuremberg Trials* (New York: Alfred A. Knopf, 1993).

11. Quoted in Jon Elster, *Closing the Books: Transitional Justice in Historical Perspective* (Cambridge: Cambridge University Press, 2004), p 90.

12. Ibid.

13. Quoted in Ian Ousby, *Occupation: The Ordeal of France 1940–1944* (New York: St Martin's Press, 1997), p 312.

14. See William Maley, *The Afghanistan Wars* (New York: Palgrave Macmillan, 2002), p 28.

15. See *Afghanistan: Conviction and Death Sentence of Former Intelligence Chief Flawed* (New York: Human Rights Watch, 7 March 2006).

16. Laurel Miller and Robert Perito, *Establishing the Rule of Law in Afghanistan* (Washington DC: Special Report no 117, United States Institute of Peace, March 2004), p 12.

17. Ali Wardak, "Building a Post-War Justice System in Afghanistan," *Crime, Law and Social Change*, vol 41, 2004, pp 319–41.

18. *Voter Education Planning Survey: Afghanistan 2004 National Elections. A Report Based on a Public Opinion Poll* (Washington DC: The Asia Foundation, July 2004), pp 14, 16, 31.

19. See Rebecca Linder, *Voices of a New Afghanistan* (Washington DC: Post-Conflict Reconstruction Project, Center for Strategic and International Studies, June 2005), pp 10–11.

20. Louis Dupree, "Post-Withdrawal Afghanistan: Light at the End of the Tunnel," in Amin Saikal and William Maley (eds), *The Soviet Withdrawal from Afghanistan* (Cambridge: Cambridge University Press, 1989), pp 22–51 at p 44.

21. See Richard Mulgan, *Holding Power to Account: Accountability in Modern Democracies* (London: Palgrave Macmillan, 2003).

22. See Timur Kuran, "Ethnic Norms and Their Transformation Through Reputational Cascades," *Journal of Legal Studies*, vol 27, no 2, June 1998, pp 623–59; and also Russell Hardin, *One for All: The Logic of Group Conflict* (Princeton: Princeton University Press, 1995).

23. Cass R. Sunstein, *Risk and Reason: Safety, Law, and the Environment* (Cambridge: Cambridge University Press, 2002), p 86 (passage co-authored with Timur Kuran).

24. See Toby Dodge, *Inventing Iraq: The Failure of Nation Building and a History Denied* (New York: Columbia University Press, 2003); Jeffrey

Record, *Dark Victory: America's Second War Against Iraq* (Annapolis: Naval Institute Press, 2004); David L. Phillips, *Losing Iraq: Inside the Postwar Reconstruction Fiasco* (Boulder: Westview Press, 2005); Larry Diamond, *Squandered Victory: The American Occupation and the Bungled Effort to Bring Democracy to Iraq* (New York: Times Books, 2005); and George Packer, *The Assassins' Gate: America in Iraq* (New York: Farrar, Straus and Giroux, 2005).

25. See William Maley, "Peacekeeping and Peacemaking," in Ramesh Thakur and Carlyle A. Thayer (eds), *A Crisis of Expectations: UN Peacekeeping in the 1990s* (Boulder: Westview Press, 1995), pp 237–50.

26. For some discussion of factors shaping foreign policy formulation within the Bush administration, see Ivo H. Daalder and James M. Lindsay, *America Unbound: The Bush Revolution in Foreign Policy* (Washington DC: The Brookings Institution, 2003); and Robert Jervis, *American Foreign Policy in a New Era* (New York: Routledge, 2005).

27. Richard A. Clarke, *Against All Enemies: Inside America's War on Terror* (New York: The Free Press, 2004), p 31.

28. See Isaiah Berlin, *The Crooked Timber of Humanity: Chapters in the History of Ideas* (London: John Murray, 1990), p vii.

Epilogue

1. See International Crisis Group, *Afghanistan's New Legislature: Making Democracy Work* (Brussels: ICG Asia Report no 116, 15 May 2006), p 10.

2. For an example of his work, see Rangin Dadfar Spanta, *Afghanistan: Entstehung der Unterentwicklung Krieg und Widerstand* (Frankfurt am Main: Peter Lang, 1993).

3. See William Maley, *The Afghanistan Wars* (New York: Palgrave Macmillan, 2002), pp 228–32; Michael Barry, *Massoud: De l'Islamisme à la Liberté* (Paris: Éditions Louis Audibert, 2002).

4. Isobel Coleman and Swanee Hunt, "Afghanistan Should Make Room for Its Female Leaders," *Christian Science Monitor*, 24 April 2006.

5. Wahidullah Amani, *Have Hekmatyar's Radicals Reformed?* (Kabul: Institute of War and Peace Reporting, ARR no 210, 6 April 2006).

6. *The Afghanistan Compact* (Kabul: Government of Afghanistan, 2006), Annex I.

7. *Afghanistan National Development Strategy: An Interim Strategy For Security, Governance, Economic Growth and Poverty Reduction* (Kabul: Islamic Republic of Afghanistan, 2006), p 61.

8. Beth Gardiner, "World Pledges $10.5B for Afghanistan Aid," *Washington Post*, 1 February 2006. By contrast, the US was estimated in early 2006 to have spent US$76 billion on military operations in Afghanistan since September 11, 2001: see David S. Cloud, "$120 Billion More Is Sought For Military in War Zones," *New York Times*, 3 February 2006.

9. *Afghanistan: Civilian Life Must Be Donor Priority* (New York: Human Rights Watch, 2006).

10. For an earlier analysis highlighting the importance of sustained commitment, see Barnett R. Rubin, Humayun Hamidzada, and Abby Stoddard, *Through the Fog of Peace Building: Evaluating the Reconstruction of Afghanistan* (New York: Center on International Cooperation, New York University, 2003).

11. Carlotta Gall, "Taliban Threat Is Said to Grow in Afghan South," *New York Times*, 3 May 2006. See also Pamela Constable, "Afghan Corps Faces a Resurgent Taliban," *Washington Post*, 10 June 2006; Carlotta Gall, "Taliban Surges as U.S. Shifts Some Tasks to NATO," *New York Times*, 11 June 2006; and *Helmand at War: The Changing Nature of the Insurgency in Southern Afghanistan and its Effects on the Future of the Country* (London: The Senlis Council, June 2006).

12. See Elsina Wainwright, *Precarious State: Afghanistan and the International and Australian Response* (Canberra: Strategic Insights no 23, Australian Strategic Policy Institute, March 2006).

13. Pamela Constable and Javed Hamdard, "Accident Sparks Riot in Afghan Capital," *Washington Post*, 30 May 2006. See also Rachel Morarjee, "Riots Breach Kabul 'Island'," *Christian Science Monitor*, 30 May 2006; Pamela Constable, "Shaken by Riots, Afghans Gripped By Uncertainty," *Washington Post*, 31 May 2006; Pamela Constable, "The End of the Kabul Spring," *Washington Post*, 11 June 2006.

14. See Seth G. Jones, "Averting Failure in Afghanistan," *Survival*, vol 48, no 1, Spring 2006, pp 111–28; Ali A. Jalali, "The Future of Afghanistan," *Parameters*, vol 36, no 1, Spring 2006, pp 4–19.

Index